Advance praise for *Strategic Execution*

"Having the best strategy is for naught if you can't execute—and then constantly adapt it. Carrig and Snell have provided an invaluable service by providing business leaders with a framework to develop, execute, and then adapt any strategy."
—Jim Barber, chief operating officer, UPS

"In a crowded landscape of books on strategy and execution, Ken Carrig and Scott Snell find a sweet spot that focuses on real-world examples and practical tools and advice for leaders to have an immediate impact."
—Daniel Marsili, SVP and CHRO, Colgate-Palmolive Company

"Ken and Scott have laid out a compelling framework for simplifying strategy and turning ideas into action. *Strategic Execution* clearly shows that the right simplified plan, organizational structure, and team, along with embracing the need to move quickly, are the all-critical components to delivering results."
—Greg Brenneman, chairman of CCMP Capital and lead board director of Home Depot

"Execution is key to organizational performance, and *Strategic Execution* presents insightful and implementable ideas to improve every organization's execution capabilities. Filled with practical examples and evidence, this is a supremely useful and readable book."
—Jeffrey Pfeffer, Stanford Business School, and coauthor of *The Knowing-Doing Gap: How Smart Companies Turn Knowledge into Action*

"The biggest challenge for any leader is twofold: setting direction and 'GSD' (getting stuff done). Carrig and Snell have laid out a comprehensive and pragmatic approach that will help any organization achieve success through results."
—David Pace, CEO and president, Jamba Juice

"This book has many important practices and examples to help all leaders better execute their strategies."
—Dennis Glass, CEO and president, Lincoln National Corporation, and Lisa Buckingham, CHRO, Lincoln National Corporation

"Carrig and Snell have executed a great book on execution! With insightful stories, useful tools, and elegant concepts, this work will help leaders master the 4 As. Any leader who wants to turn strategy into action will find these ideas invaluable."
—Dave Ulrich, Rensis Likert Professor, Ross School of Business, University of Michigan and partner, The RBL Group

"*Strategic Execution* substantially raises the profile of execution, while simultaneously serving up a very crisp model to immediately improve your organization's execution capacity—and overall performance."
—Kevin Cox, CHRO, General Electric

"This book is about how to approach execution following a simple framework but with many tools, surveys, and assessments to assure the work gets done."
—Dick Antoine, retired CHRO, Proctor & Gamble and past president, National Academy of Human Resources

"This is a must-read for leaders in the digital age. Business disruption is everywhere, and the businesses that will thrive will be those that can implement complex strategies swiftly and effectively. This book gives a blueprint to do just that."
—Eva Sage-Gavin, senior managing director, Accenture Global Talent & Organization

STRATEGIC EXECUTION

STRATEGIC EXECUTION

Driving Breakthrough Performance in Business

**Kenneth J. Carrig and
Scott A. Snell**

STANFORD BUSINESS BOOKS
An Imprint of Stanford University Press • Stanford, California

Stanford University Press
Stanford, California

Printed in the United States of America on acid-free, archival-quality paper

Special discounts for bulk quantities of Stanford Business Books are available to corporations, professional associations, and other organizations. For details and discount information, contact the special sales department of Stanford University Press. Tel: (650) 725-0820, Fax: (650) 725-3457

Library of Congress Cataloging-in-Publication Data

Names: Carrig, Ken, author. | Snell, Scott, author.
Title: Strategic execution : driving breakthrough performance in business / Kenneth J. Carrig and Scott A. Snell.
Description: Stanford, California : Stanford Business Books, an imprint of Stanford University Press, 2019. | Includes bibliographical references and index.
Identifiers: LCCN 2019011273 (print) | LCCN 2019016892 (ebook) | ISBN9781503609792 (e-book) | ISBN 9781503603592 (cloth: alk. paper)
Subjects: LCSH: Strategic planning. | Organizational effectiveness. | Performance.
Classification: LCC HD30.28 (ebook) | LCC HD30.28 .C3725 2019 (print) | DDC658.4/012—dc23
LC record available athttps://lccn.loc.gov/2019011273

Typeset by Newgen in Minion Pro 11/15

Cover design: Christian Fuenfhausen

Dedicated to Tom and Theresa Carrig and to John and Clara Snell, leaders from whom we first learned the discipline of getting stuff done. Produce!

Never mistake motion for action.
—Ernest Hemingway

CONTENTS

ACKNOWLEDGMENTS

How would you choose which flower in the garden is the most beautiful, as they all add to its collective splendor? So, too, does each of the people listed below who together helped bring this book to fruition.

Our thanks go to:

- First and foremost, our wives and best friends, Lisa Carrig and Marybeth Snell, who as always were not only great supporters of us throughout this endeavor, but were kind enough to preread our chapters and even kinder to say they liked our work.
- The five CEOs, the senior leaders, and the companies, who were instrumental to the content. We hope we captured well what you all have accomplished.
  - SunTrust: Bill Rogers, Margaret Callahan, Mark Chancey, Sue Mallino
  - Vail Resorts: Rob Katz, Blaise Carrig, Mark Gasta, Jeff Klum, Lynanne Kunkel
  - Marriott: Arne Sorenson, David Rodriguez, Ty Breland, Karl Fischer, Jim Dausch, Shannon Patterson, Adam Malamut
  - UPS: David Abney, Teri McClure, Jim Barber, Alan Gershenhorn, Scott Price, Dean Foust, Theron Colvin
  - Microsoft: Satya Nadella, Kathleen Hogan, Scott Guthrie, Stacy Elliott, Chuck Edwards, Joe Whittinghill
- The great team that helped us develop the manuscript: Katie McBride, our professional reviewer, helped make the manuscript more readable. She made the suggestions we needed to hear and was extremely flexible to the changing deadlines that occurred during book writing. She became a partner and friend. We'd also like to thank Steve Momper, Darden Business Publishing, who gave us great advice and direction.

And thanks also to Shannon Weisbrodt, who transcribed hours and hours of interview data.

- Our CHRO friends who agreed to read parts of the book and provided great, timely, and useful feedback. They are Bill Allen, Dick Antoine, Kevin Barr, Lisa Buckingham, Kevin Cox, Daniel Marisili, John Murabito, and Laurie Siegel.

- Steve Catalano and Margo Fleming from Stanford Publishing, who provided encouragement throughout the book writing process and kept us on track.

Our hope is that this book will make a positive difference in enabling leaders to create and sustain excellent organizations. We did our best to provide meaningful stories and a framework that has been tested and can be customized to the needs of your company. It is in the spirit of learning that we started this journey and brought you this book. We now also welcome your feedback concerning the 4A Framework and how it might be used in your organization. You can reach us at snells@darden.virginia.edu and kencarrig@gmail.com.

Again, thank you.

STRATEGIC EXECUTION

1 THE CEO'S TOP CHALLENGE

EVERY GOOD BOOK begins with a compelling premise. Here's ours: The greatest challenge of CEOs and top management teams is helping their organizations execute better. This challenge either supersedes or is instrumental to most any other issue these executive teams face, whether it's achieving better financial performance, market growth, sustainability, innovation, or leading through disruption. To achieve any of those outcomes, we know they first need to crack the code on execution.

It's not as easy as it might sound. As we began discussing the issues with a broad group of colleagues and business leaders, their interest in the topic was overwhelming. They were searching for answers. And what surprised us is that they weren't sure if they were framing the question the right way. So we've been on a quest to better understand the challenge of execution, and find the best ways to address it.

Here's how it all began: A few years ago, during a strategy review process at SunTrust, our analysis of the banking financial services industry revealed something interesting. Strategy alone did not differentiate high- from low-performing firms. Instead, the true differentiator between winners and losers turned out to be how well the strategy was executed. The data on this were pretty compelling, and the fact is we weren't doing all that we should.

Although the financial services industry has always been competitive, the financial crisis of 2008 and the years of the Great Recession placed unprecedented pressure on traditional players, including SunTrust. A confluence of legislative, regulatory, economic, and technological changes—as well as continued consolidation—drove mounting challenges to profitable growth. During the crisis, as revenues declined and the costs of meeting regulatory requirements rose, many banks experienced a spike in their efficiency ratios (a critical measure of performance defined as noninterest costs divided by gross revenue). A high ratio is a bad thing, and SunTrust's was among the worst in the industry.

Despite improvements in subsequent years, SunTrust still lagged behind other competitors. The bank's regional scale alone was not enough to explain its disadvantage. Compared to competitors of similar revenue and headcount, SunTrust fell in the lowest quartile in efficiency. The bank's strategy wasn't to blame either. If anything, SunTrust had some strategic advantages in terms of its reputation and the markets it served. That bank simply wasn't as productive as its peers. And wasn't executing like it should.

Bill Rogers became CEO in 2011, and immediately brought the leadership team together in a three-day offsite to undertake a comprehensive review of the bank to determine the best path forward for SunTrust. The team used the time—away from the daily whirlwind—to do a frank self-evaluation and thorough investigation of the underlying causes of the performance gap. At first, the temptation was to rebalance the strategy and business mix—after all, the financial crisis exposed some deep concerns in industry fundamentals.

But the team ultimately had an epiphany of sorts, and we learned some important lessons in the process that changed the way SunTrust approached strategic reviews from then on. SunTrust needed to pick a place in the market where it could win, and then focus intensely on becoming the best at that.

Period.

Like many companies, SunTrust had been spending too much time analyzing the "what" of strategy—the goals, targets, objectives, and metrics of the business. Nothing wrong with that, of course, but by comparison, there wasn't enough time spent on the "how" of the business. Not enough time on the "who," the "when," and ultimately, the "why." Collectively, these questions define the domain of execution.

And that's where SunTrust was missing the mark. Over several years, Rogers and team refined the bank's approach to strategy execution to integrate and balance these priorities for execution excellence. The approach became essentially an operating framework for the strategy sessions. And more than that, it became a key approach to running the business every day, baked into the culture.

SunTrust's results were impressive. The company's overall performance improved from last quartile to median performance or better in all key indicators. It achieved a substantial improvement in its efficiency ratio, decreased costs, and enhanced customer value. As a result, SunTrust achieved market-leading performance in shareholder value among the top ten banks.

But even with this progress, there was less celebration than you might imagine. Why? Because the job is never done. As SunTrust improved, it continued to look for additional performance breakthroughs. As Rogers put it, "From a performance standpoint, we've clearly outperformed. You know, we're not there [yet]. I want to be best. You know, we're not best. We are really better. We're a lot better."

THE BIGGER STORY

In this book, we'd like to tell more of SunTrust's story. And of other companies like it. The reality is that SunTrust's journey is not particularly unique. Winning in business and sustaining success is complicated and difficult. Nobody is immune from the challenges of execution. Even perennial powerhouses like General Electric, Boeing, or even Apple stumble from time to time. The key is how they respond.

How pervasive is the execution challenge? A recent Conference Board Survey of CEOs identified execution capability as the number one concern facing today's business leaders. The joke was that execution is so important, it was ranked number one AND number two in the survey. Another study found virtually the same thing. More than four hundred global CEOs in Asia, Europe, and the U.S. ranked executional excellence at the top of the list of some eighty different challenges, surpassing innovation, geopolitical instability, and top-line growth.[1]

The data on this are fairly compelling, and there is good reason for concern. Here are just a few more data points:

- Morgan, Levitt, and Malek reported that "90% of companies consistently fail to execute strategies effectively."[2]
- Kotter reported that 70 percent of all strategic initiatives fail because of poor execution.[3]
- A Booz and Company study found that employees in three out of every five companies rated their organization weak at execution because strategic and operational decisions are not quickly translated into action.[4]
- A study by Bain found that only 15 percent of companies have truly high performance organizations (another 62 percent were adequate, and in 23 percent of the cases, the organization actually depresses performance).[5]

Add it all up, and the conclusion seems to be glaringly obvious: (1) execution is important both strategically and operationally, (2) many of us, regardless of industry sector, need to be better at it, and (3) poor execution is a leading cause for concern among CEOs.

But rather than fall into the trap of "admiring the problem" and not addressing the solution, we followed up on these studies with our own investigations. We convened a series of C-suite roundtables with senior executives from a variety of companies. American Express hosted one roundtable in New York City; Marriott hosted one in Washington, DC; McDonalds hosted one in Chicago; Hewlett Packard hosted one in Palo Alto; and SunTrust hosted one in Atlanta (see the list of participating companies in Table 1.1).

We invited executives from a range of industries to get a cross-section of perspectives from manufacturing, service, technology, health care, government, etc. Most of the participating companies were fairly large (Fortune 500) and recognized for success in their industries, so our sample was skewed a little bit by that. But we made no effort to simply select and benchmark top firms, even though many were the best at what they do. Rather, we wanted a diverse set of companies with a range of experiences, who could share their successes and struggles, what they had tried, what had worked, and what they continue to learn.

WHY SO MUCH INTEREST?

The roundtables generated a lot of interest and enthusiastic participation from senior executives. It became clear to us that the goal of execution excellence was something most organizations were trying to achieve, and something few believed they had truly mastered.

In part we wanted to use these forums to road-test our ideas, as a sort of reality check. But generally we just listened. We had learned a lot from the SunTrust experience, but we wanted to absorb how others saw the problem and how they approached the challenges of execution.

Many participated because they wanted to learn as well, and they came with more questions than answers. The groups were kept small, and everything was confidential, not for attribution beyond the room. Because of those stipulations, the conversations were frank, unvarnished, confronting at times, and honest. These were smart people with vast experience and enormous responsibility, who took the time to share with one another and offer their insights. Perhaps most telling, there was less "advice giving" than one might have imagined. No one claimed to have all the answers.

The session discussions centered on three primary issues with regard to execution capability: (1) Business Context and Challenge—what were their priorities for execution, and why did it matter in their business? (2) Framing and Capability—what were the critical drivers of execution capability, and how did they determine which elements mattered most for improving performance? (3) Action—how did they sequence their actions and investments to improve execution capability and performance?

We invited participants to first engage in a divergent process, laying out the many factors underlying execution successes and failures. Then we moved toward convergence, urging the participants to combine and compartmentalize related factors to consolidate and synthesize their lists to the most important drivers of execution excellence.

And we learned a ton.

TABLE 1.1 Participating Companies

Abbott	Ericsson	McGraw-Hill Companies
Accenture	General Dynamics	McKesson
Ally Financial	General Electric	Microsoft
American Express	Gilead	Moody's Corporation
BAE Systems	Hewlett Packard	Motorola
Blackstone Group	Hyatt Hotels	Munich RE
Bloomin' Brands	IBM	Newell Rubbermaid
Boeing	Intel	Northern Trust
Broadridge Financial	ITW	Pfizer
Carter's	Kaiser Permanente	Safe-Guard Products
CDW	Kelly Services	Sears
ChangAn Motors	Laureate	SunTrust
Chick fil-A	LinkedIn	Symantec
Citigroup	Lockheed Martin	UPS
Coca-Cola	Marriott	U.S. Army
Delta Airlines	Maximus	Vail Resorts
Equifax	McDonalds	Workday

WHAT HAVE WE LEARNED?

We learned a number of things from these roundtables, and heard several common themes repeated from one session to another. Subsequent to that, we created an online diagnostic survey, and have since worked with a broader set of executive teams in Europe, Asia, and North America to help them work through the execution challenge. And we have taken a deeper dive into five "spotlight" companies to learn from their experiences, to ground our research in practice, and to shine a light on the perspective from their CEOs and leadership teams.

"Execution Is Absolutely Critical."

OK, not exactly an earth-shattering insight. The problem isn't that executives fail to recognize the importance of execution; they do. And they echoed what we had seen in the banking industry. One executive observed, "Five percent of the challenge is strategy; 95 percent is the execution." Others seemed to think that proportion was about right.

Why? Because strategy is only an idea, a hypothesis, until it is actualized. And in many industries, there is actually minimal differentiation in the strategies firms pursue. Think about your own industry. Our bet is that your competitors know what you and others are doing, and can replicate (at least in principle) many elements. Academic theories of "sustainable" competitive advantage are waning, because the evidence is clear that advantage based only on strategy is usually temporary.

In our experience there are two primary reasons why execution is recognized as the bigger challenge. First, execution includes myriad elements that need to occur in practice, coming together in real time, not just in theory or an analyst's report. The complexity and contemporaneous nature of the job make execution more difficult. Second, and related, it simply takes more time. Adjustment, iteration, and constant attention, refining and building capability, drives results.

Senior executives often want to delegate execution to others, while they attend to bigger issues. Don't make that mistake. The truth is, execution is the big issue.

Now, two minutes for rebuttal by the opposing bench: One CEO in our roundtables admonished the group that it's not *all* about execution. He had been recently hired to turn around a foundering company in a tough retail market, and we understood where he was coming from. "If you have a bad strategy, it doesn't matter how well you execute," he argued. Fair enough, and we wouldn't disagree. A bad strategy is equally fatal.

But a good strategy without execution is no better. As Procter and Gamble's CEO, A. G. Lafley, put it, "The only strategy your customer or competitor ever sees is the one you execute." We suspect that part of the reason why execs are so emphatic about the importance of execution is they live with the very tangible consequences of a gap between aspiration and reality, between strategy and performance. Performance is their report card.

"The Approach Is Elusive."

Although we can easily find agreement that execution is critical, there's far less agreement on what is required to achieve it. Former Honeywell CEO Larry Bossidy noted that people believe they understand execution—"It's about getting things done," they said. But when asked *how* they get things done, "the dialogue goes rapidly downhill."

Researchers at McKinsey found similar divergence; they asked senior executives, academics, and colleagues in the consulting world for their insights, finding no agreement about the keys to execution.[6]

That's a puzzle. Why are the requirements for execution so elusive? Why is it that so many executives sense what's missing but are unsure of what to put in its place? They see the hole, but not the fill. They feel the pressure to close the gap between strategy and performance. They know they need to make a change and deliver results, but are not clear on what changes are needed most. Or which ones will have the biggest effect.

Execution is elusive because it has so many moving parts. There's a significant gap between the intuitive idea of "getting [stuff] done" and the realities of many interlinked and mutually dependent elements. In our roundtables, we'd begin by asking executives to list just the most important drivers of execution. Within minutes they would generate lists of a couple of dozen factors, all of which are "critical." Timelines, goals, metrics, processes, leadership, culture, communication, deliverables, etc.—the lists go on.

The truth is that there are probably a thousand things that need to be attended to. But if there are too many variables to consider, too much to synthesize, too many prescriptions, execution gets bogged down in its complexity. Mark Morgan and his colleagues at Stanford cautioned that complexity has to be managed or strategic execution will deteriorate into a game of "whack-a-mole" where organizations respond to one urgent problem after another as they each raise their ugly head.[7]

Execution is elusive because some of its key requirements are intangible. Leaders of high-performing organizations understand the palpable yet almost ethereal nature of execution excellence. "You can feel it"—you can feel it when it's there, and you can feel it when it's not. Great execution has energy. It generates momentum, it's accelerating, empowering. It's even fun. Poor execution is frustrating, confusing, chaotic, deflating. You can feel the drag on the organization. And that kills performance.

Getting it right is a little like harnessing the aerodynamics of flight. The Wright brothers' most difficult challenge at Kitty Hawk was not getting their "flyer" up in the air. That actually was the easy part. It was getting the right balance of lift, drag, propulsion, pitch, roll, and yaw. They had to control the combination of those intangibles by changing things that were, in fact, very tangible. The design of the wing, the engine mount, the steering mechanism, and so on. Same goes for strategy execution. Leaders need to control the flight in their organizations by affecting a complex of intangibles such as culture, commitment, alignment, and purpose. And they need to do it by redesigning tangible factors including structure, processes, technology, talent, and their own behavior. Lots of pieces that all need to be in sync. Not an easy task.

"Execution Is Not Just Implementing a Plan."

Curiously, many of our discussions with business leaders about the requirements for execution begin with their circling the issue, explaining what execution excellence is NOT. Part of the reason they do this, we guess, is that over time they've learned that traditional assumptions about what's required for execution have been challenged or refuted.

Among the first things they note is that execution is not simply implementing a plan. The world is not neat and linear; it's messy and deviating. In a rational world, we want to logically equate execution and strategy implementation. It only makes sense. Frankly, we expected that most of our conversations would start there. But they didn't.

There are important management tools that make execution more systematic and methodical. "But it's not simply project management," they say. When talking about what needs to go right—and what often goes wrong—participants in our roundtables tended to emphasize a much broader scope of interacting challenges related to blending organizational design, culture, operations, technologies, and human resource management. They also talked about their fledgling efforts to build a metrics model in order to calibrate how all these elements come together.

In a related way, execs also remind us that execution is not a "once and done." It is continuous and unending, not a discrete or episodic event. It manifests from a complex of interactive decisions, investments, and actions over time. It becomes, in the best cases, an enduring way of working, baked into the culture of the organization.

As we were conducting the roundtables, one executive from American Express was adamant that we should avoid conceiving of execution as "the Big Curtain Up," where all the players know their lines, each part is choreographed, the music starts, and the show begins. What he meant by that is that too many organizations see execution as laying out a plan (the script), assigning responsibilities (casting), allocating resources (choreography), and launching the effort (curtain up). His point was that American Express, like many other companies, faces a more dynamic world, and the key to execution is more capacity for adjustment and change, flexibility, versatility, and agility.

"There Must Be A Better Way."

Executives often reluctantly admit that they don't have a clear way forward, and their frustration is evident. Even some of the very best companies in our sample acknowledged that they don't have a concise way to frame the requirements of execution, a means for assessing it, or a methodology to focus on its improvement. Without that, it's difficult to make progress. As James Richardson put it, "We have many useful frameworks for formulating business strategy, i.e., devising theory of how to compete. Frameworks for strategy execution are comparatively fragmented and idiosyncratic."[8]

Yes, there is a better way. Our purpose in writing this book is to lay out the requirements for execution excellence. For those in positions to make a difference, this book frames an approach that focuses attention on the key challenges as well as the principle considerations and practices that lead to breakthrough performance. It also provides a set of invaluable tools for translating strategy into the realities of day-to-day business performance.

Our journey to understand the phenomenon revealed dozens of potential things to consider, and seemingly just as many people with a point of view on the subject. To be sure, we are not presuming to have all the right answers, or answers that are right all the time. However, based on our experience, we distilled the lessons learned from senior executives to provide a succinct set of insights, practices, and interventions.

OUR APPROACH

When we began talking with our publisher about this book, we spent time discussing what makes our approach different. What distinguishes our work from others who speak to the same or similar issues? Since Peters and Waterman's classic work, *In Search of Excellence*, the volumes of books sold on the topic of execution and performance has been substantial. That's good news—there's a strong foundation on which to build.[9]

Our approach is to focus on the things that matter most. While there are many considerations that need to be attended to, the strong advice we got was to derive an approach that is tight, highlighting the most crucial elements, and robust with regard to impacting performance. Don't try to boil the ocean. Think of this akin to the Pareto 80/20 rule, where 20 percent of the factors account for 80 percent of performance.

How can you narrow the aperture on execution excellence? The approach cannot be overly elaborate, or frankly no one will (be able to) use it. One of the primary reasons that organizations fail to execute in an integrated way is that they haven't developed a truly transportable rubric for action. As a practical matter, CEOs don't need or want "sixty-eleven" things to attend to. As one exec reminded us, "CEOs have only a few levers they can pull, but they are big levers." In our experience, winning organizations are more often those that focus on perfecting those precious few elements that make the biggest difference in driving performance.

Our approach is to focus on improvement, not perfection. Although perfection may be the goal, it's not a one-step hop to get there. We'll highlight areas where companies have made the greatest gains and found a step change in performance. We concentrate on lessons learned and high-impact zones where companies have moved the needle in improving their execution capability. We haven't sought to simply benchmark the most profitable, good-to-great companies and then provide a post hoc prescription of how one might emulate them. Others have done that, and the approach is compelling. But history suggests it has a limited shelf life—five years from now, the list of best-in-breed companies may well have changed, and advice based only on their performance will have lost some credibility. Instead, the companies we highlight are interesting because they are world class, but not because they are perfect. They have learned important lessons in their own journey of execution and have developed an approach that allows them to continually improve. They acknowledge they have faltered at times, and they have gotten better.

As an aside, have you ever noticed that coaches often have greater fondness for their most improved players, even if the MVPs score more points? And just as importantly, others often learn far more from the most improved players in order to raise their own game.

None of the companies with which we have worked assert that they have it all figured out, or that they have achieved a threshold of execution excellence (even if they have). The executives approached our discussions with great humility. Their reticence to prescribe is not born of false modesty. These executives point to areas where their progress is evident and where their investments pay dividends in terms of enhanced performance. Throughout the book, they share lessons learned rather than claiming victory. We like their approach.

Our advice is to concentrate on ways to get better and better. Work to close the gap between where you are and where you need and want to be. In that regard, achieving execution excellence is much like developing your core capabilities. Work in a concerted way to strategically upgrade the underlying skills, values, processes, and structures that underlie those capabilities and combine to drive performance. That's the heart of where execution occurs, and that's how organizations excel.

With these points in mind, our book is intentionally written to achieve tripartite goals of simplicity, accuracy, and generalizability. In science, researchers often make trade-offs among parsimony, internal validity, and external validity. And although inevitably it is impossible to have all three, we would observe that some competing volumes gave up where we have not. Our work is grounded in research, giving us greater confidence in the accuracy and internal validity of our observations. We have reinforced those observations by taking a deeper dive into the practical experiences of five spotlight firms. And we have included a broad array of firms and industries to improve the generalizable inferences and external validity of our work. And perhaps most importantly, we have kept you—the reader—foremost in mind. The value of our work is inherently dependent on how usable it is to you.

GROUNDING THE IDEAS IN PRACTICE

To illustrate the principles and practices of execution excellence, we share the experiences of CEOs and top leaders from our five "spotlight" companies: Marriott, Microsoft, SunTrust, UPS, and Vail Resorts. These executive teams have been generous with their time, giving us open access and engaging in some very forthright discussions. They have agreed to share their approaches to execution; what works, where they have struggled, and what they continue to learn. Not only do these case studies enrich our understanding of the phenomena, but they also illustrate how other organizations have made progress in their approach to the challenges of execution. You won't just hear our ideas; you'll hear theirs.

Marriott International

Marriott International is one of the most admired names in the hospitality industry. The company's roots go back to 1927, when J. Willard Marriott and his wife, Alice, opened a nine-seat A&W root beer stand in Washington, DC. Since that day, the company has grown to become the largest hotel chain in the world, with a portfolio of more than 6,400 properties and over one million hotel rooms, spanning 126 countries and territories. With the acquisition of Starwood Hotels and Resorts in 2016, the company includes among its 30 leading hotel brands Ritz Carlton, St. Regis, JW Marriott, Westin, Sheraton, Courtyard, and Residence Inn. The company has more than 140,000 employees and a market cap over $50 billion, and is recognized for its excellent business operations, standards of service, and reputation as a top employer. Imagine the challenge of providing premier hospitality services on that scale and scope.

Arne Sorenson is only the third CEO in Marriott's history, and the first who is not a Marriott family member. Prior to joining Marriott, Sorenson was a partner with law firm Latham & Watkins in Washington, DC, and in the early 1990s was hired by Bill Marriott to be the corporate attorney. "At some point I found myself listening to Arne's ideas with more than ordinary interest," Marriott said. "He had a good grasp of the company's strengths and weaknesses, a feel for the future of the travel industry and a sense of direction that impressed me and others. . . . Arne definitely stood out. He also seemed to 'get' our values and culture—key for anyone who might lead the company someday." Sorenson took on a number of different roles, broadening his experience across the enterprise by building relationships from the board to the rank and file, which is critical in Marriott's service-oriented culture. In 2009 he was promoted to president and chief operating officer, and when Sorenson became Marriott's CEO in 2012, he not only inherited responsibility for a global organization, but he also became a steward of Marriott's legacy.[10]

Marriott's execution challenge: Integrate Starwood into its family of hotels in order to create a unified portfolio. Sorenson and team are very optimistic and see this as part of its strategy to innovate the customer travel experience.

Microsoft

Microsoft was the brainchild of Bill Gates and Paul Allen. Founded in 1975, the company's fortunes rose considerably in the 1980s through its partnership with IBM, as its MS-DOS and later Windows operating system soon dominated the PC industry. In 1990 the company released Microsoft Office, including Word, PowerPoint, Excel, Outlook, and more. This suite of application software further solidified Microsoft's position as the standard bearer in personal computing. Since that time, the company has grown and diversified beyond the software market to include hardware such as Xbox and Surface, and has made a number of acquisitions including Skype for $8.5 billion in 2011, Nokia mobile for $7.2 billion in 2014, LinkedIn for $26 billion in 2016, and GitHub for $7.5 billion in 2018. Today the company has over 135,000 employees and a market cap of more than $800 billion.

Satya Nadella is only the third CEO of Microsoft, and has big expectations placed on his shoulders. During his short tenure, Nadella has made sweeping changes in the company to rekindle its spirit of innovation, learning, and growth in order to reinvigorate the company's passion for excellence in a new era of computing. Respected for his personal approach and insight, Nadella grew up in Hyderabad, India, and emigrated to the U.S. to pursue a master's degree in computer science at the University of Wisconsin–Milwaukee and then an MBA from the University of Chicago. He joined Microsoft in 1992 after a short stint at Sun Microsystems and rose through a series of key positions in both consumer- and enterprise-focused business groups, before taking on the leadership of Microsoft's Cloud and Enterprise group. It was that role that perhaps best prepared him to become CEO in 2014.

Microsoft's execution challenge: Complete its metamorphosis from a desktop software company to an experiences and services company. Nadella and team are working to transform the culture to inspire innovation as they pursue their mission to "empower every person and every organization on the planet to achieve more." They see a unique opportunity to do so in a cloud-first and mobile-first world.

SunTrust

You already know something of the SunTrust journey. The company's story began on September 21, 1891, when the Georgia General Assembly granted a charter to the Commercial Travelers' Savings Bank (later renamed the Trust Company of Georgia). In 1919, the Trust Company's president, Ernest Woodruff, and W. C. Bradley led a group of investors who bought Coca-Cola for $25 million, and the bank helped underwrite Coca-Cola's initial public offering. The bank grew through a series of acquisitions, and in 1985 the Trust Company of Georgia and SunBanks of Florida merged to form SunTrust Banks, Inc. Based in Atlanta, the company grew into one of the largest financial services companies in the U.S., with assets of $206 billion, serving 4.8 million households and business clients, and providing deposit, credit, trust, investment, mortgage, asset management, securities brokerage, and capital market services.

CEO Bill Rogers began his career in 1980, after graduating from the University of North Carolina with a degree in business. Bill joined

SunTrust's commercial banking division, and over the years held a series of positions in corporate and commercial banking, corporate finance, retail banking, private wealth management, and mortgage loans, prior to being named president in 2008 and chief operating officer in 2010. After taking the CEO post in 2012, Rogers led a significant transformation of the company. His focus on execution was particularly significant, and as part of that he built on SunTrust's client-first culture and increased focus on operating returns and efficiency. Under his leadership, SunTrust became a more purpose-driven company, widely recognized for its dedication to Lighting the Way to Financial Well-Being for the people, businesses, and communities it serves. Bill continues to be a champion for the company's philanthropy and volunteerism and serves on a number of local and national organizations.

SunTrust's execution challenge: While the bank made great strides in executing its strategy over the past decade, Rogers and the SunTrust team faced a new challenge from larger banks (i.e., Bank of America, Wells Fargo, JP Morgan, etc.) that have made substantial investments in technology, ushering in a new era of mobile banking. To compete at scale, and counter with its own technology investments, SunTrust recently agreed to a merger of equals with BB&T, making it the sixth largest U.S. Bank. Not coincidently, SunTrust's superior execution capability made them an attractive partner to BB&T, and increased the prospects of a successful merger. The execution challenge now is to achieve alignment in this new enterprise, blend the organizations, access new talent, build an integrated architecture, and achieve better agility through its digital transformation.

United Parcel Service

United Parcel Service (UPS) delivers an average of 19 million packages each business day for 1.6 million shipping customers to 8.7 million receivers. Just ponder that for a moment. Nineteen million packages every business day. Back in 1907, James Casey and Claude Ryan borrowed $100 to start a bicycle messenger and delivery service in Seattle, Washington. Today, UPS is a global leader in logistics, offering a broad range of solutions including the transportation of packages and freight, the facilitation of international trade, and the deployment of advanced technology to more efficiently manage the world of business. It employs more than 444,000 people and has a market cap over $100 billion. Its global transportation network serves more than 220 countries and territories, and includes a ground fleet of more than 108,000 vehicles and an air fleet of more than 500 aircraft operating major air hubs in Louisville, Kentucky; Cologne, Germany; and Shenzhen, China.

CEO and board chairman David Abney began his career in 1974 as a part-time package loader in a small facility in Mississippi while working on his degree in business at Delta State University. Like many other executives who thrived in the UPS promote-from-within culture, David worked his way up to become president of UPS International, and then chief operating officer, overseeing logistics, sustainability, engineering, and all facets of the UPS transportation network, before assuming the role of CEO in 2014. During his tenure, Abney has led a UPS transformation, expanding its global network, capabilities, and investments in technology for a new era of business.

UPS's execution challenge: Transform the organization through technology investments in order to enhance its "smart logistics" network. Abney and team are working to simultaneously achieve greater efficiency in its global business model while taking advantage of new, profitable growth markets.

Vail Resorts

Vail Resorts is the leading operator of world-class ski resorts and alpine hotels in the U.S., Canada, Australia, and throughout the world. Its portfolio of 15 ski resorts includes Vail, Beaver Creek, Breckenridge, Keystone, Park City, Heavenly, Northstar, Kirkwood, Stowe, Whistler Blackcomb (Canada), Perisher (Australia), as well as the luxury hotel chain RockResorts. In the early 1960s, Pete Seibert and Earl Eaton, both ski patrol guides at Aspen, set off to pursue their dream of creating the next great ski mountain, and in 1962 started Vail Associates. The company went public in 1997, and since 2010 has been growing significantly through acquisitions, transforming the nature of competition in the entire ski industry.

Rob Katz became CEO of Vail Resorts in 2006 (and Chairman in 2009). Prior to that he worked for Apollo Management, the private equity firm that brought Vail out of bankruptcy and set it on its current track. Rob's passion and ambition for Vail is clear, and he has been widely recognized as a Global Game Changer (*Forbes* 2017), one of Most Creative People in Business (*Fast Company* 2017), and Transformational Entrepreneur of the Year (*Ernst & Young* 2016). During his tenure, Vail Resorts has been recognized as one of America's Best Employers (*Forbes* 2016 and 2017), one of the World's 50 Most Innovative Companies (*Fast Company* 2016), and one of the World's Most Innovative Companies in Travel (*Fast Company* 2017). Throughout this book, we will share more of the story of Rob's impact on the company, and the industry.

Vail Resort's execution challenge: Build a world-class organization while redefining customer engagement and the face of competition in the ski industry.

DO YOU SEE YOURSELF?

If you picked up this book, you probably have some responsibility for executing strategy. Or soon will. Given the pervasiveness of the execution challenge, the audiences for this book are many and varied. Can you see yourself in any of these stories?

For senior-level executives, we provide perspective from those at the top of their firms. The case studies of Marriott, Microsoft, SunTrust, UPS, and Vail Resorts are framed by their CEOs and leadership teams, and we have used their priorities to help set our agenda. Our objective is to channel *their* thinking and share *their* lessons learned.

CEOs and top leaders value the accessibility of our approach in that it captures, in a concise way, the key priorities for addressing the execution challenge. We hope you do, too. In the next chapters, we introduce an actionable model for excellent execution that we call the *4A framework*. We also explain how the four elements work together, reinforcing and supporting one another. Although there is much complexity underlying the framework, we purposely designed it to capture the key lessons in a way that emphasizes usability.

Throughout the book we introduce a set of self-assessments and a template for developing more robust data analytics, to help you calibrate where you stand in the execution framework. We hope that you use these diagnostics to engage in your organization and to work with your colleagues to refine your priorities for improvement. When we use these tools with management teams, it sparks a conversation—and debate—and it helps them focus on the most important courses of action. Where they disagree with one another, they confront the realities of those differences. And where they agree, they move toward devising a plan for improvement.

This book includes a set of application guidelines to ground the ideas and establish a playbook for practical intervention. While the process starts at the top of the organization, we know execution happens at every level. Middle managers are often the ones most frustrated by execution challenges, as they have the difficult task of translating strategic imperatives into operation actions. They are also the ones who make it happen—and have responsibility to drive performance through others. We often say to our students and clients, "Some of you may be responsible for formulating strategy, but *all* of you are responsible for executing it."

A word of caution: In an effort to find a better way, executives routinely hire consulting firms to evaluate their organization, diagnose performance problems, recommend solutions, and devise a course of action. There's real value in that, because external advisors can provide a different perspective, proffer new ideas, and generate loads of supporting data. But after making that investment (and enduring the invading horde of experts), these companies discover that improvement can only come from within. You can't farm it out. The CEO and leadership team own execution, and while others have their roles, it cannot be simply delegated. Success requires executives to stay engaged, leading the process as a collaborative endeavor for which they are accountable.

2 THE 4A FRAMEWORK

Focus Resources and Energy

FOUR PRIMARY FACTORS determine execution excellence. The more we engage with companies on their own execution journeys, the more our work has zeroed in on these four factors. Where companies have problems, these are the most troublesome areas. And when they achieve performance breakthroughs, these are the areas that drive improvement. We refer to them as the 4 As: Alignment, Ability, Architecture, and Agility. Here is how we define them:

- *Alignment:* Everyone is focused on the same strategic outcomes, with shared understanding of their roles, commitment, and accountability to deliver exceptional performance.
- *Ability:* The organization has the leadership and talent needed to perform at a high level, as well as the ability to collaborate effectively across the enterprise to achieve high-priority strategic outcomes.
- *Architecture:* The organization's design creates clear authority structures, supports efficient workflow, and enables effective decision making to drive performance.
- *Agility:* There is dynamic capability to respond quickly to emerging opportunities, stay in front of change, reallocate resources, and foster ongoing organizational learning.

THE 4A FRAMEWORK

No matter the industry, organizational success depends on developing a user-friendly framework to guide the firm's collective efforts to achieve strategic goals. The 4A model provides that framework, integrating Alignment, Ability, Architecture, and Agility. We've seen the power of the framework in numerous organizations.

For example, while UPS has an enviable reputation for operational excellence, the company continually strives to get better, approaching improvement as a disciplined process. "We have just really started to put a rigor to [our journey]," said UPS International president Jim Barber. "Linking the four As in UPS has a firm process built around it, as strong and as robust as the way we take business models to the world." As he explained, "The ability to launch [our] strategy, move it into the field, execute it . . . ask yourself how good and how robust a process you have around that. Because the four As work on the development of strategy, and they work on the execution of strategy."

Throughout the book, we'll discuss how the 4A framework can help you see your business through the lens of execution requirements and how it can serve as a platform for engaging others in important discussions to prioritize action and intervention. This framework is especially important as companies grow and evolve. The practices may change, but the principles remain the same. Marriott's CEO Arne Sorenson put it this way, "You know, thirty years ago, Bill Marriott could virtually visit every hotel. He could review every hotel's budget in the entire company one at a time." But as the company has grown, that is just not possible. Marriott developed a framework to execute strategy at every level. "We've become very good at using these different channels to communicate and much more structured in communicating well-defined priorities, and these get communicated from the top all the way to the bottom," Sorenson explained.

Now we must offer one proviso. Frameworks are useful, but they can become sterile if they remove leaders from the real work of execution. Vail Resorts CEO Rob Katz reminded us that execution occurs mano a mano. "This happens one person to one person." he said. "It's not that

I've come up with a policy or best practice. Every company has that. Where the difference shows up is how each leader actually drives these points home to their people and that is one to one."

With the challenges of execution as backdrop, and the real interest among CEOs and executive teams to make a difference, let's take a quick look at how we organize this book. Chapters 3–6 are deep dives on each element in the 4A framework: Alignment, Ability, Architecture, and Agility. Each chapter covers the key questions that executives ask, barriers to execution, and the focus areas to guide action and improvement. These points are summarized below in Table 2.1. In addition, we also highlight the key points of each chapter.

Alignment

Alignment conveys the deceptively simple notion that execution depends on everyone working together toward the same goal. In our meetings with CEOs and leadership teams, they consistently and emphatically stress that alignment is both the most important factor in execution, and the first that needs to be addressed in order to improve performance. It is the *sine qua non* of execution; without it, they say, nothing else much matters.

Why? Just think about it. Organizations exist only because people can accomplish more working together than on their own. When aligned, organizations bring disparate elements together into a unified whole. Just like a laser that concentrates energy to amplify the intensity of light, alignment channels effort and resources toward key outcomes. It provides clarity of purpose and direction, momentum to overcome inertia, a focus for decisions and actions, and resilience in the face of change or disruption.

However, in large and complex organizations, where managers and employees often work in silos, their attention becomes compartmentalized, or rather "departmentalized." As you might expect, they often lose perspective on how their efforts work in service of the whole. When we ask them about their company's strategy, they often give us only generalities or platitudes. When we push a little more to be concrete, they default to "This is what I do, this is my job." There's often a substantial

TABLE 2.1 Four Elements of Execution

	Key Questions	Barriers	Focus Areas
ALIGNMENT	• How do you ensure that everyone is focused on the same strategic intent? • Have you built a high-performance culture with shared aspirations and expectations? • How do you instill a sense of mutual accountability for results?	• Distraction, diversion of attention away from goals • Dispersed resources that diminish impact • Flagging engagement	• Strategic intent • Shared performance expectations • Accountability for results
ABILITY	• Do you have the right leadership team, working as a strong unit? • If talent is your most important asset, what does your investment portfolio look like? • Where is collaborative capability needed?	• Chronic talent shortage • Reactive approach and short-termism • Insufficient talent needed to pursue growth goals	• Strong leadership bench • Talent capacity • Collaborative capability
ARCHITECTURE	• How well understood is your organization's operating model? • How do you ensure your infrastructure propels performance rather than impedes it? • Do processes and systems enable or inhibit workflow and strategy execution?	• Repeatedly letting the customer down • Working in silos or poor decision structures • Flying blind without required information	• Clear operating model • Streamlined organization • Intelligent systems support
AGILITY	• Is your organization able to respond quickly, or are you blindsided by change? • How do you support organization learning to drive innovation and knowledge sharing? • How well have you developed ability to redeploy resources quickly?	• Chin-down management • Threat-rigidity • Inertia and momentum	• Situational awareness • Organizational learning • Dynamic capability

gap between their understanding of the requirements of strategy and their own work. Misalignment becomes the norm, not the exception.

It is therefore a constant challenge to emphasize the mission-critical elements that unite the organization toward its strategic purpose and to work across the enterprise to achieve those outcomes. An important part of alignment is clarifying with others how work for which they are accountable leads to those strategic outcomes, how overall success is attributable to them.

In Chapter 3, we lay out the serious threats to alignment—what pulls organizations apart, diverting collective effort and traction. Then we tackle the most important practices and approaches for achieving alignment. This includes clarifying the overall strategic intent of the organization: its purpose, identity, and direction. We then share the approaches CEOs use to elevate shared expectations for performance, or what Doug Ready and Emily Truelove refer to as "collective ambition," rooted in the culture of the organization. And we provide guidance for helping you ensure that your organization builds a system of mutual accountability that is both explicit with regard to performance outcomes and implicit in the shared values and standards of your organization.[1]

Ability

The second element in the 4A framework is Ability.

In any endeavor, whether business, sports, or the arts, great execution requires great skill. No matter how fine the composer or how beautiful the score, the performance depends on the mastery of artists working together to bring life to the music.

Have you ever noticed how many corporate annual reports begin with a pro forma statement such as "People are our most important asset." As clichéd as that may sound, we don't doubt the veracity of the sentiment. Many of our discussions with CEOs begin with their sincere recognition of the importance of leadership and talent, and a reminder that every single employee makes a difference when it comes to execution. It's where they spend a preponderance of time, and it's one of the areas they, frankly, worry about the most.

Interestingly, what begins with a discussion of alignment, and the goal of everyone pulling together, often evolves to a deeper discussion of leadership ability and talent. When it comes to strategy execution, the challenge is to get the most out of their human assets. This isn't just a focus on productivity but also attracting, developing, and deploying the best human capital; raising skill levels; and making sure that the types of knowledge, skills, and abilities are appropriate for the task.

And as you might imagine, great talent is in short supply. In Chapter 4, we'll address some of the reasons why firms come up short when it comes to talent and ability, a characteristic we refer to as the "talent syndrome" that plagues a lot of firms and prevents them from executing as they could. We'll also share some of the key lessons for boosting talent capacity, beginning with the importance of getting the right CEO and senior leadership team. From there we will share some of the insights about building a differentiated talent model, identifying critical positions, and the key approaches for developing a robust pool of talent. Like any capital investment, the "make or buy" decisions for talent require tough choices about where payoffs will be greatest. Because HR budgets are often the first to be cut in difficult times, fewer dollars means more scrutinized investment. The priority with regard to execution is generating more high performers, particularly in critical roles.

We also see collaborative capability as an important "talent multiplier" leveraging the knowledge and skills of each person to help others perform more effectively. In this regard, collaborative capability is essential for execution. In our discussions with leadership teams, they emphasize the importance of teamwork and the willingness to collaborate (an element of alignment). But they quickly move beyond that point alone and emphasize the *ability* to collaborate effectively, which is itself a skill particularly in broader networked organizations.

Improving collaborative capability is not an easy undertaking, but can be crucial for achieving execution excellence. We look at this on three levels. First, there are structural elements that either bring people together or make collaboration more difficult. These need to be identified and addressed. Second, there are cognitive elements that either create mutual understanding and knowledge sharing or impose an intellectual divide. These need to be attended to as well. And third, there are dispositional or affective elements that either engender trust and reciprocity or provoke the tendency toward office politics and division. These need to be surfaced and addressed. We'll share some of the ways executives have worked to build their collaborative capability, why it is important to them, and the effect it has had on their strategy execution and performance. Along the way, we'll note the connections that collaboration has to our prior discussion of Alignment, and we'll also use this to introduce the next section on the design of the organization, Architecture.

Architecture

The third element of the 4A framework is Architecture. The design and configuration of your organization, as well as its underlying infrastructure, processes, technologies, and controls constitutes the domain of organization architecture. Your organization's design makes a big difference in terms of reliability, scalability, and continuity of performance. In terms of strategy execution, the organizational architecture is critical for managing communication, resource flows, information availability, decision making, and processes that propel the organization forward. Getting the design right, and ensuring good alignment and ability, can transform organizations and lead to breakthrough performance.

Unfortunately, we have found that organization architecture often does just the opposite. Harvard Business Review's Advisory Council of senior executives agreed that organization architecture is often their biggest obstacle to strategic execution. The very structures, processes, and systems that are supposed to enable work often are the most entangling impediments to effective execution. Poor architecture slows down decision making in a morass of reporting relationships, regulations, approvals, and other bureaucratic tendrils. It confuses and impedes progress through inefficient resource flows, process inefficiencies, conflicting priorities, and finger pointing. And it obfuscates rather than elucidates decision making with incomplete or distorted information.[2]

In our experience, the effect of organizational architecture on strategy execution can be positive or negative, but it is rarely neutral. Why? Because architecture represents the synchronization of many elements of the organization. Structures, processes, systems, and controls need to work together as a mutually reinforcing system. When they do, that system hums, and performance gets better. When they don't, things can quickly bind up as though gears in a motor were grinding with one another.

When the elements of architecture all come together, it can literally change the game. Here's an example. In the 2013 America's Cup sailboat race, Larry Ellison and Team Oracle USA changed the architecture and design parameters of the sailboat, and it transformed the entire sport. Rather than using the traditional mono-hull sloop with canvas sails, Ellison's design team created the AC72-class wing-sail catamarans. These 86-foot leviathans had a solid wing-sail that worked much like an airplane wing, giving the boats new capability. The combination of the wing-sail, the multihull design, and two carbon-fiber dagger boards under each hull enabled the boats to hydrofoil—completely lifting the boats out of the water so they could literally fly above the surface at speeds reaching 50 mph (45 knots). Ironically, Oracle Team USA was not as proficient with the AC72 design as Team New Zealand, who for generations had been masters of competitive sailing. Oracle fell behind 8–1, but the team collected and analyzed race data every night and made design changes, process changes, and tactical changes to improve its execution. In one of the great comebacks in sailing history, Oracle won the final series 9–8 by mastering the new way of sailing. The new architecture had redefined America's Cup sailing.

You may not think of your organization as an America's Cup race. But you can see the analogy. In a very real sense, your organization's architecture places an upper limit on execution capability, performance, and how you are able to compete. In Chapter 5, we'll discuss some of the chief concerns you may have with regard to your own organization's architecture, and you may see symptoms you have in common with other firms. More importantly, we also address what you can do about it. Some of the biggest derailers of strategy execution are inherent in the design of the system. But the good news is that many firms have achieved breakthrough performance by modifying their organization architecture.

We begin by discussing ways to clarify your operating model—the set of end-to-end core capabilities that drive customer value, as well as the processes, systems, skills, and structures that comprise it. Your operating model serves as an architectural blueprint for performance and helps make priorities for execution more explicit. Then we focus on ways to streamline your organization's architecture, simplifying structures, improving processes, as well as clarifying roles, responsibilities, decision rights, and authority. This includes building lateral connections across the enterprise to improve collaboration and joint decision making. And importantly, there is a social architecture that coevolves with the formal architecture. Informal relationships, interaction patterns, and cultural norms can support or subvert the goals of execution. Finally, we'll provide some examples of ways that top management teams have invested in technology, data analytics, and artificial intelligence to aid problem solving and decision support.

Architecture not only can be powerful and enabling, it can be beautiful and inspiring. In many cases, architecture determines how high we can go, how far, and how fast. Keeping in mind it's only one of our four execution factors, its importance for strategy execution cannot be overstated.

Agility

There is an apocryphal story of Albert Einstein giving his assistant an exam to distribute to graduate students. "But Professor Einstein," she said, "these are the same questions as last year." Einstein allegedly replied, "It's all right, the questions are the same, but the answers are different."

The same can be true for strategy execution. In high-velocity environments, questions about growth, profitability, innovation, and execution may remain the same. But the answers about how to achieve them are changing rapidly. In such a dynamic environment, the ability to respond and adapt is critical for achieving organizational goals. Or as our friends in the military often remind us, "No plan survives first contact with the enemy." Agility is important because the battlefield keeps changing. The key to execution increasingly depends on being agile, nimble, and responsive in the face of change and discontinuity.

Agility has both reactive and proactive connotations. From a reactive standpoint, agility is the capacity to respond quickly and adjust to external disruption, to cope with exogenous change, and to adapt to potentially unforeseen circumstances. In these instances, companies are forced to play defense, and execution is focused on urgent, sometimes difficult change. For example, when U.S. auto companies were caught off guard by the popularity of Japanese hybrids, they had to scramble to introduce models that could compete with the likes of Toyota, Nissan, and others. Some companies respond better than others, and building the capacity for reactive change is an important aspect of organizational agility.

But agile execution also has a more proactive connotation. Companies work to get out in front of change, to create disruption for others, to build an organization that is capable of continuous learning and innovation. The same car companies that found themselves playing catch up with hybrid technology are now investing ahead of the curve to drive the future adoption of all-electric and self-driving vehicles. General Motors, for example, has emerged as a top leader in autonomous vehicle development and announced plans in 2017 to launch more than twenty new all-electric, zero-emission vehicles by 2023. GM CEO Mary Barra has invested significant time and resources to build a culture capable of embracing and driving this change. "It's about creating an environment for collaboration and giving people tools they need to work effectively. How can we make sure you really have a work environment that's enabling and empowering, instead of constricting?"[3]

At about the same time, Bill Ford Jr., Ford's executive chairman, announced the creation of Team Edison, a special unit that combines technology, product development, marketing, and advanced manufacturing to accelerate the company's "clock speed" in developing electric and autonomous vehicles. To further accelerate change, Ford decided to carve out its autonomous-vehicle program into a separate wholly owned company, unencumbered by the larger organization. As Sherif Marakby, chief executive of Ford's Autonomous Vehicles, said, "What's important is having the focus of this team to think big, move fast and in a very agile way."[4]

Despite these efforts, Tesla passed both Ford and GM to become the most highly valued car company in the U.S. (market cap over $60 billion). Its top position was not because of the number of cars Elon Musk's company was selling, which was substantially less than traditional competitors, but because investors at the time saw Tesla as better positioned to drive innovation and change. Still, there were lingering concerns about Tesla's ability to deliver on that potential. The challenges of execution never go away.[5]

There are a few important lessons we've learned about agile execution. Remember our colleague at American Express who warned that execution today is not just a "Big Curtain Up." He was right. In Chapter 6, we focus on ways to help your organization respond better, adapt more quickly, and redeploy assets to drive performance. Ironically, one of the most common inhibitors of agility is our own approach to execution, a phenomenon we call the "Execution Paradox." In an attempt to drive better performance and maximize efficiency, many organizations create a situation where change and adjustment are more difficult. The harder they work, it seems, the more challenging it is for them to see the need for change, to flex, adapt, and adjust appropriately. Does that ever happen to you? Do you find yourself blindsided by change, flatfooted, and unable to stay out in front?

Part of the challenge is creating the capacity to see what's coming, or what's possible. Some of the most agile organizations have developed situational awareness that gives them deep insights to customer needs, and broader peripheral vision of what's happening in the marketplace and external environment. We'll cover some of the ways you can build situational awareness in your organization by empowering others to help surface potential opportunities and leveraging the collective wisdom of those around you.

Agile organizations are consummate learners. They are less likely to "bet the farm" on big gambles, but continually undertake a series of small wagers, recoverable investments that help them learn, explore, and influence the future. What they learn, they share broadly within the organization, rather than falling into the trap of hoarding knowledge or compartmentalizing information. Finally, we'll cover some of the key lessons learned about building "dynamic capability," and share approaches you can use to increase your capacity to reallocate and redeploy resources in ways that strengthen the core of your organization while investing in the future.

Although experience suggests that agility is a bigger priority for some firms than others, no one is ignoring it. In even the most traditional industries (as we saw with U.S. car companies) building the capacity to respond quickly and consistently is a requirement for execution excellence.

One last point; of all the elements in the 4A framework, agility is the newest and least well understood. Organizations who for years tried to create stability and eliminate variation as a precondition for execution excellence are having to rethink their approach. The change has not come naturally. More on that in Chapter 6.

THE INTERACTIVE SYSTEM

Each of the four elements of execution is important in its own right. Alignment, Ability, Architecture, and Agility are the drivers of breakthrough performance. However, to function effectively, they need to work together as a system, supporting and reinforcing one another to strengthen their overall impact. Because of their nature, they will influence one another on their own, but for maximum effect they need to be managed jointly. This is perhaps an intuitive idea and consistent with your own experience, but also worth making explicit before we go forward.

For example, strong alignment and purpose make it easier to attract and develop talent, build a top-notch leadership team, and focus collaborative capability (Alignment → Ability). Conversely, when alignment decays, talent scatters and collaboration dies. In just the same way, strong alignment helps establish priorities for the organization architecture and even compensate in places where/if that architecture may fall short (Alignment → Architecture). For example, if your executive team galvanizes action around the organization's strategic intent, it has the effect of anchoring your operating model, helping to clarify authority structures, roles, and decision rights. It also gives a focal point for process (re)design, systems reengineering, information access, etc. Finally, alignment helps to reinforce agility, providing a source of integration and stability in the face of change (Alignment → Agility). It not only gives the organization its core foundation for springing to action but it also serves to unite the organization in those inevitable cases where agility leads to temporary divergence and variation.

Take a moment to think about how the other elements of the 4A framework interact with one another in your organization. Ability,

Architecture, and Agility all have those potentially synergistic effects. Taken together, they can strengthen each other. Just as importantly, if managed poorly they can eliminate or diminish the effects of the other three. We've seen some deadly combinations, say for example where poor Architecture fractures Alignment, or where Ability gaps hamstring Agility. You see our point—it's an interactive system. Throughout the rest of the book, and particularly in Chapter 7, we focus on both the independent effects of the four As, and also discuss their interactive impact as well.

Now let's step back from the framework for just a moment. There are a couple dimensions that distinguish the four As from one another, and at the same time bind them together. We find it useful to think of execution excellence fundamentally as *leveraging the firm's resource base to energize performance.* As shown in Figure 2.1, the 4A framework combines two categories of resources, human capital and organizational capital, and two types of energy, potential and kinetic. Let's take some time to consider each dimension.

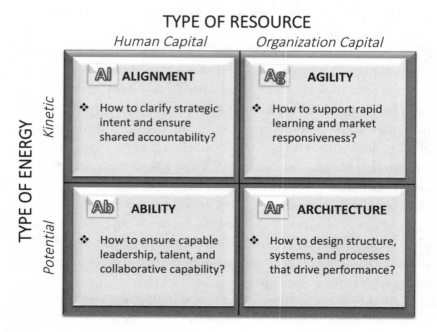

FIGURE 2.1 The 4A Framework

Resources: Human and Organizational

Strategy execution is inherently a process of developing and deploying resources in service of key organizational outcomes (i.e., growth, profitability). Some of those resources are obviously human, and some are organizational. For example, firms use technology, processes, systems, information, as well as financial resources. Throughout the book, we emphasize that achieving executional excellence depends on identifying, investing in, and allocating resources that will have the greatest effect on performance.

Of the many, find the few. And focus there. That axiom is going to ring true in our discussion of Alignment, Ability, Architecture, and Agility. As management guru and professor Michael Porter so famously said, "Strategy is about making choices." The same can be said of strategy execution.[6]

During the 1990s, New York City police commissioner Bill Bratton was able to achieve a dramatic turnaround and breakthrough performance of the New York City Police Department by focusing critical resources on those key areas that would drive out crime. With limited manpower and resources and budget cuts, Bratton resisted the normal temptation to scale back his aspirations. Instead he concentrated on specific crime zones and felonies that could achieve the greatest marginal improvement. In addition, he focused on key human resources—his precinct commanders—and held them publicly accountable for delivering results and sharing their approach with others. He focused on political resources the same way, identifying key constituencies who might be the greatest supporters and those who might be the strongest detractors. Within two years, and without any budget increase, Bratton transformed New York City into the safest metro area in the U.S., decreasing felony crime by 39 percent, murders by 50 percent, and theft by 35 percent.[7]

There's a two-part lesson here. On the one hand, improving your organization's ability to execute depends on finding those potentially limited resources that will give you most leverage. Where's the biggest bang for your buck? On the other hand, or the other side of your hand, we would suggest that resource allocation be directed at those few areas that are holding you back the most, what Eliyahu Goldratt referred to as "theory of constraints." In his book *The Goal*, Goldratt posited that any manageable system is limited in achieving its goals by a very small number of constraints. By identifying the constraint and restructuring the rest of the organization around it, redeploying resources, you improve throughput capacity, and elevate performance.[8]

Energy: Potential and Kinetic

The second dimension underlying the 4A framework is energy. Although you likely refer to people and organizations as "resources," we'd guess that you're less likely to see them as sources of energy. But ask any leader with responsibility for strategy execution, and he or she will tell you, "Resources are important; managing energy is essential." During one of our roundtables, one executive advised us, "There's perhaps no asset more critical to execution, nor more undervalued, than the management of energy." Organizations are systems, and like any system it must generate more energy than it expends in order to survive. In his work with senior teams, Jim Clawson emphasized that "leadership is about managing energy, first in yourself and then in those around you." Rob Cross and colleagues found through their research that some of the highest performers in organizations are what they called "energizers," individuals who communicate a compelling vision, create opportunities for others to contribute, actively seek input, and facilitate progress toward goals. Energy is contagious and affects everyone around us. In the best cases, the entire organization can be affected positively.[9]

In Chapter 1 we noted that execution is made more difficult by the fact that some of its requirements are intangible. This is especially true of energy. How do you manage it? Let's start with the concepts of *potential and kinetic energy*. Potential energy is stored energy, latent within an object, based on its makeup and design, as well as its relationship to other objects. Think about a set of pool balls, carefully racked together on the table prior to a game. If you've seen what's possible, you know the enormous potential energy stored in that composition. Kinetic energy is energy released and put into motion. This energy can be transferred from one object to another, much the way energy passes from the pool stick, to the cue ball, to the set of racked balls as they expand outward. It can be startling. (Ken often demonstrates this principle to Scott when we play a game of pool, and typically exacts a small fee for the trouble.)

How does that apply to business? Organizations are powered by the potential energy of leadership, talent, structure, and processes. They also deploy the kinetic energy of having everyone aligned and able to flex, respond, and evolve. Let's look at this in the context of the 4A framework. Ability and Architecture are sources of potential energy—the human and organizational capacity to achieve more. Execution excellence is latent in both these resources. At the same time, organizations leverage Alignment and Agility as sources of kinetic energy—vitality that activates and propels your organization forward. Alignment energizes commitment, momentum, and enthusiasm through a shared sense of purpose and strategic intent. Agility energizes discovery, learning, and innovation releasing energy from the core. Of course, the distinctions between potential and kinetic energy are not as discrete as they might appear in the 2x2 square in Figure 2.1. Just as the four elements interact, the flow of energy intermingles among them as well.

To see how this looks in practice, consider DuPont's development and commercialization of nylon. DuPont began research on nylon back in 1930. Its genesis came out of a company redesign, restructuring the chemical department into several small research teams to focus on pure science that might eventually have industrial application. This was important for generating the autonomy to pursue new innovation. One team, headed by Wallace Carothers, worked on polymer research combining chemical compounds into new synthetic materials. His team worked for over nine years on nylon prototypes, repeatedly testing new possibilities, deepening their expertise, honing their process, and mastering a steep learning curve with colleagues across other departments.

Think of these investments as building future capability—potential energy that would power subsequent performance. Producing nylon required a complex manufacturing process, using high-pressure chemistry, which ultimately became the foundation for industrial production still used today. DuPont's production facilities eventually were capable of spinning up to 12 billion pounds of nylon annually. Even before the product was available to the public, nylon fiber was marketed to consumers, building excitement and demand for the first manmade textile fiber. It was first used during World War II to make parachutes and tents. And then, postwar, when it finally became widely available to the public, demand skyrocketed and nylon revolutionized the hosiery industry.[10]

The DuPont example helps to illustrate the role of potential and kinetic energy in strategy execution. Building capacity, expertise, and organizational capability are critical for increasing the upside potential for excellence. And then leveraging that potential through the power of shared purpose, collective ambition, and organizational learning helps to accelerate momentum, responsiveness, and breakthrough performance.

A LOOK AHEAD: HOW TO USE THIS BOOK

With the 4A framework as background, we use the next four chapters to go deeper into Alignment, Ability, Architecture, and Agility and the role each plays in addressing execution challenges.

Each chapter is written using a similar format. First, we begin each chapter with a set of scenarios that give you a quick glimpse into specific execution challenges of Marriott, Microsoft, UPS, SunTrust, and/or Vail Resorts. These scenarios help ground the key elements of the 4A framework in their experience.

Next, we detail some of the symptoms of poor execution; places where organizations get hung up with Alignment, Ability, Architecture, and Agility. The point is to give you a sense of how these challenges may manifest in your own organization, and how to diagnose underlying performance problems. These symptoms help tee up the next section called "What Can You Do?"

Each chapter contains three main priorities or principles for improving execution that have been derived from research, executive roundtables, and company case studies. For each of these three main priorities, we give a few more recommended actions, and we include extensive examples and advice from executives at Marriott, Microsoft, UPS,

SunTrust, and Vail Resorts to illustrate the concepts and practices. Each company and leadership team has its own approach for addressing the execution challenges. Our goal is to show that while the requirements and principles of execution are common, how they are applied can be different. Indeed they must be different to meet the specific strategy, culture, and competitive environment of each organization. While you can learn a good deal from the company examples, your approach may be somewhat different, too.

At the end of each chapter, we include a section called "Where Do You Stand?" This provides a quick self-assessment that summarizes the key takeaways from the chapter, and helps you calibrate where your organization is on that dimension. (As a cheat sheet, we also provide the complete self-assessment diagnostic of all four As as an appendix at the end of the book.)

Finally, in Chapter 7, we go into more depth about using the 4A framework with your own team. The chapter outlines how to contextualize the approach within a broader business review, providing advice about how to assess your execution capabilities and how to build a playbook for intervention and action planning.

Now let's begin with our first deep dive in the 4A framework: Alignment.

3 ALIGNMENT

The Imperative of Shared Intent

IN 2008, SunTrust CEO Bill Rogers regularly visited regional branches of the bank to talk with employees, to hear what they were thinking and how they were feeling. In his view, keeping in touch with front-line "teammates" (the SunTrust term for its employees) was important to the company's client-first culture. As he recalled, during the height of the financial crisis,

> I was out at one of our branches, and a teammate who'd been with us a long time told me, "When I leave here, I take my name badge off when I stop at the grocery store so people won't know that I work at a bank." This was more a function of what the industry was going through than our company. Nonetheless, I never want teammates to feel that way—ever. I want them to be proud of the company they work for, be purposeful in their work, and I want them to be able to connect their work with the purpose and goals of the company. This is what we're here to do.

The challenge for Rogers was one of accentuating SunTrust's *mission*. He had to elevate that purpose, to help employees connect with it, and understand how they contribute to it. This inspired him to ensure his executive team was aligned in their purpose and approach to get there.

Microsoft's story was somewhat different. Some believed the company had lost its way when Satya Nadella became CEO in 2014.[1] The company had grown into a large and, some say, lumbering organization that had trouble focusing. As Chief Human Resources Officer Kathleen Hogan described, "We would go into meetings with so many things to cover. . . . The company's working on all these things." With so many initiatives, everything became a priority. And as they say, when everything is a priority, nothing is a priority. Nadella was called to craft a clearly focused *direction* for the company, and an aligned, integrated strategy to match.

When Rob Katz became CEO of Vail Resorts in 2006 he undertook an acquisition strategy that grew the company from a handful of independent ski resorts in Colorado to a portfolio of more than twenty resorts across three countries. *Integrating* all those parts into one enterprise was his challenge. Customers loved the idea that they could pay one price for an Epic Pass and ski any of the company's resorts around the world. The problem was that Katz's initial leadership team wasn't prepared to deliver on this vision. As Katz put it, "Even when everyone has the best of intent, there are different perspectives on how to actually get from point A to point B. And it's very easy to quickly find yourself out of alignment where people are spending time and effort on things that are not actually helping the company succeed. In a competitive environment, that is a huge disadvantage."

These stories reveal different facets of the alignment challenge, and how they are critical to firm performance. As we noted in Chapter 1, CEOs see alignment as both the most important factor in execution and the first that needs to be addressed. When organizations are aligned, the rich diversity of talents, resources, experiences, and opportunities can come together with focused intensity to achieve greater performance.

Yet in our experience, many companies fail to follow through deeply enough to ensure that total alignment actually occurs. It's a classic case of "easier said than done." It takes serious work to get there. And most CEOs acknowledge that alignment is never fully achieved—it is an ongoing challenge. Worse, misalignment feeds on itself in a vicious cycle where distractions lead to more disintegration. Misalignment can kill an organization because of divergent actions and interests, conflict and dispersion, diffusion of effort, and waste and frustration at every level.

To explain this, refer to your high school physics book and the *law of entropy*. All systems are predisposed toward disarray and randomness, giving off or dissipating energy along the way. It takes far more energy to keep a system together, aligned and organized, than to have it disperse. Think about how quickly and effortlessly a set of dominoes falls versus the time it takes to stack them. Think about the rapid demise of the Roman Empire or the Soviet Union. Think about how easily your closet becomes disheveled versus the effort to keep it neat. Each of these examples, big and small, illustrates the pull of entropy. Organizations are no different.[2] And the more complex the system, the more the tendency toward dispersion and misalignment.

What might this look like in your organization, and what can you do about it? The first step is to identify the potential signs or sources of misalignment and their underlying causes. Perhaps you'll recognize some of the following common symptoms.

SYMPTOMS OF MISALIGNMENT

Let's start with a simple analogy. Have you ever driven a car that's out of alignment? It's no thrill ride, right? The car pulls to the left or right, the steering wheel vibrates, the tires squeal. You grip the steering wheel, trying to keep things going straight, manage the resistance, and decrease the wear and tear on your vehicle. It's frustrating and exhausting. And dangerous.

While it may be more subtle at first, organizational misalignment is just as debilitating. Employees at all levels must overcompensate, oversteer, and often decelerate to cope. While not as obvious as a shaking steering wheel, there are some recognizable symptoms when an organization lacks alignment. Let's look at this and dig deeper.

Symptom #1: Do You Get Sidetracked, Distracted, and Diverted?

Does your organization get distracted and diverted from priorities that matter most? Instead of focusing on mission-critical objectives and goals, organizations often get sidetracked, sometimes by very attractive "shiny objects." This tendency came up often in our senior executive roundtables. Many leaders acknowledge the gravitational pull of the latest industry trend, their reactionary response to competitor dynamics, their compulsive fixation on monthly sales or quarterly earnings reports, all diverting attention from long-term priorities and strategic investments. In their book, *Strategy That Works,* Paul Leinwand and Cesare Mainardi reinforce the importance of addressing such diversions in order to build better strategic alignment: "It is all too easy to continually shift your focus—to deal with exigencies and never quite build the capabilities you need."[3]

Some would argue that McDonalds was distracted for several years in its fruitless efforts to woo health-conscious customers (who almost never ate there). In the process of trying to broaden its base by expanding its menu to salads, wraps, and the like, McDonalds neglected its core—making great burgers. New, "better burger" chains began pulling in customers with gourmet, made-to-order burgers and quick, casual service. After losing an estimated 500 million U.S. orders over a five-year period, the company announced it would get back to basics, reembrace its identity as a fast-food chain, and worry less about appealing to a customer group they were never likely to win over. The lesson learned? According to Lucy Brady, SVP of corporate strategy, "We don't need to be a different McDonald's, but a better McDonald's."[4]

Disciplined alignment toward what is truly most important acts as a guardrail from getting sidetracked. In racing, they say "the car goes where your eyes go."[5] If your organization chases one fad after another or can't help lurching toward some new opportunity, those diversions may be a symptom of misalignment. That can hurt execution.

Symptom #2: Are Your Priorities and Resources Too Dispersed?

A related symptom of misalignment is if your organization is trying to do too many things at once. The dispersion of priorities, and the scattering of resources, can lead to diffused impact. When senior leaders are unable to align around a few key priorities, they often take a "peanut butter approach" and spread their resources too thin. The effect of this is to accomplish many things with little impact. Lots of motion, but not much progress. In their book, aptly named *Execution: The Discipline of Getting Things Done*, Bossidy and Charan cautioned, "A leader who says 'I've got ten priorities' doesn't know what he's talking about—he doesn't know himself what the most important things are. You've got to have these few, clearly realistic goals and priorities, which will influence the overall performance of the company."[6]

Having too many priorities is like a stream of light that is broadly diffused: it may provide no useful illumination. Managers will often rationalize that their pursuits are justifiably important (divisional sales, operational targets, etc.), but the organization will have lost its focus. As one executive told us, "There are always good initiatives and business opportunities that pop up—and they may make sense in themselves. But the organization gets too complicated." A critical task of the senior leadership team is to eliminate these otherwise good opportunities that would dilute the organization from its core focus.

A decade ago, AstraZeneca was lagging the pharmaceutical industry in R&D productivity. Its investment in research was high, but its record of bringing new drugs to market wasn't. CEO David Brennan and his team concluded the company was trying to compete in too many different therapeutic areas, the effect being too many development priorities, dispersed resource allocation, and limited impact. After a thorough portfolio review, the company decided to focus on unmet medical needs that had highest prevalence and matched AstraZeneca's capabilities. Anders Ekblom, head of global medicines development, said, "We had to make some tough choices. My analogy is a bit like a freeway. When you have a freeway which is in a traffic jam, if you add more cars into it, it just slows down even more. If you take a number of the cars away, suddenly the traffic flows freely." After the company trimmed its development portfolio, resources were allocated more effectively, collaboration across projects improved, and R&D productivity jumped. AstraZeneca's success at bringing new drugs to market rose, and revenue more than doubled.[7]

The lesson here? By focusing on less and avoiding dilution, your organization can achieve more. As Stephen Covey put it, "You have to decide what your highest priorities are and have the courage—pleasantly, smilingly, unapologetically—to say no to other things. And the way you do that is by having a bigger 'yes' burning inside."[8]

Making the tough strategic calls and aligning around a few key priorities prevents managers from making endless tradeoffs and compromises. It also helps prevent silos—a major challenge in a multitude of organizations. Without a clear, aligned mission, departments and business units often fill in the blanks, defining their own priorities and allocating scarce resources to work that may not serve the best interests of the enterprise. At an operational level, these silos result in unhealthy internal competition and conflicting interests. At best, they work well independently and generate pride only within each team. At worst, they create fierce rivalries that suboptimize performance. Perhaps you've seen instances where employees develop more loyalty to their team than their customers and the overall organization.

And while silos and resource allocation problems have been a documented difficulty for decades, the challenge is still vexing—especially in large, complex companies.

Symptom #3: Is Engagement Flagging?

Still a third symptom that your organization may have an alignment problem is if it is losing traction, spinning its wheels, losing drive and forward momentum. The disconnect between leaders and the led is often glaringly apparent, and when it happens employees may become frustrated, discouraged, even cynical, and start to disengage.[9] If they begin to believe the organization has lost its way, its sense of purpose or direction, they may get disheartened.

If employees observe a lack of clarity or authenticity among senior leaders who don't tackle the big issues, they may become skeptical and "dial it back," simply doing their job in a pro forma manner. And if they believe that their views are inconsistent with leaders, they may avoid confrontation and just keep their heads down, hoping that this too shall pass. When that happens, organizations can quickly lose momentum, dissipate energy, lose capability, and start to decay.

Take the example of Nissan Motors. During the 1990s, Nissan went through a decade-long decline that seemed irreversible. A series of three

CEOs tried in vain to increase productivity, eliminate waste, improve quality, and boost financial performance. But nothing seemed to work. Nissan's slide continued, and employees seemed resigned to the company's fate. There was a growing disconnect between what the CEOs wanted and what the employees would deliver. Enter Carlos Ghosn, the new CEO who came over from Renault. He took three key steps to reengage his organization. He reduced his leadership team from forty-three to nine to get tighter alignment, eliminated entitlements like lifetime employment, and created cross-functional teams to identify and solve key business challenges.

Ghosn's actions addressed Symptoms 1 and 2 by driving focus and collaboration. But he really sought engagement, challenging the cross-functional teams to focus on becoming "a world-class automotive company." Instead of dictating a turnaround strategy, he empowered his organization to devise one.

Ironically, their solutions were not dramatically different from the previous CEOs. But the effect was different. Within two years, Nissan was profitable again and back on a growth trajectory. Allowing the enterprise to develop and own their solutions was key to executing them.

WHAT CAN YOU DO?

If you recognize any of these symptoms, or aspects of your organization in these vignettes of McDonalds, AstraZeneca, or Nissan, you may have an alignment problem. But, you needn't wring your hands. As they say, recognizing the problem is the first step toward a solution. The good news is that despite the many challenges of alignment, real gains can be made. We saw this at Marriott, Microsoft, SunTrust, UPS, and Vail Resorts.

Our research and their examples demonstrate alignment can be improved when organizations do three things:

- Establish a clear strategic intent (the "why" of their existence)
- Generate shared expectations for high performance (the "what" they're aiming for)
- Instill mutual accountability for results (the "how" they know they are doing it)

These bullet points may make the ideas seem deceptively simple, but they can be quite challenging to enact. Let's take a deeper look at how you can enact these three "to dos" in order to make a difference.

ESTABLISH A CLEAR STRATEGIC INTENT

Step one to gain better alignment is to get everyone on board through a compelling focus on strategic intent. Why? A clearly articulated strategic intent can energize your organization around an ambitious vision of the future. Interestingly, evidence suggests that it often inspires the organization to set off toward a goal that, at the time, they may not be fully capable of achieving. But it engages collective ambition and higher aspiration. It can be a stretch experience for sure, but one that provides the "emotional and intellectual energy for the journey to the future."[10] In fact, McKinsey research has shown that the financial performance (EBITA) of firms was almost twice as likely to be above the industry median when people were clear and excited by the company's direction.[11]

When done well, the process of defining the organizational purpose actively engages leaders and others to focus on the essence of their success, energizing and clarifying the value of their collective vision. It empowers everyone to recognize their own contributions to that vision. A clear strategic intent helps to orient the organization, providing what we might call a "shared dominant logic" for sensing, framing, and responding to the world. It answers the big question of "why?"

Does your organization have a clear strategic intent? Is it understood and embraced by everyone from the CEO to the rank and file? Achieving this clarity is more difficult than many imagine. Two decades ago, Michael Traecy and Fred Wiersema wrote their book, *The Discipline of Market Leaders*. Their findings were sobering: the vast majority of executive teams they studied were unable to articulate their value proposition succinctly.[12] Our experience is that the same is true today. Without a clear strategic intent, it's difficult to establish a focal point for collective action and performance.

Check yourself on the following questions:

- How well is our strategy understood and supported by all managers?
- Are our strategic goals clearly prioritized by our leaders and regularly communicated throughout the enterprise?
- Does our executive team model all the behaviors necessary to translate strategy into performance?

The CEOs in our profile companies routinely ask themselves these questions. When they don't like their answers, they engage their leadership team to make the changes required to improve across their company—enabling both horizontal and vertical alignment.

Does Strategic Intent Unify Your Team?

In complex organizations, the day-to-day operations of independent business units and corporate functions often lead to competing priorities and fragmentation. To be fair, our narrow, siloed perspective is not necessarily wrong, but incomplete. Truth as we know it can eventually become biases inviting disagreement and conflict across departments, staffs, and regions.

Individual managers often pursue ends within their staffs or operating units that are both worthy and relevant to the organization. But without integration across their effort, to reconcile different capabilities, perspectives, and priorities, the opportunity for greater achievement is lost.

But please don't miss the point here—the goal is to integrate, not eliminate, the differences. Each unit brings something unique and important. The confluence of ideas and experience is critical. Ultimately, the focus must be on connecting all departments, regions, etc. to a shared vision—an enterprise perspective—so they don't suboptimize performance.

SunTrust: Clarify your purpose—Why are we here, whom do we serve? Let's return to Bill Rogers's priority at SunTrust. He wanted to align everyone in the entire company behind a shared purpose. Here's how he described his challenge. "Early in my career, a colleague told me the CEO has two jobs: to bring clarity from complexity, and to bring purpose to the work. If you keep those two things in mind, the doors

SunTrust: Translate your why, what, and how. Bill Rogers and his team worked to create touch points for aligning purpose and performance at every level of the bank. They instituted quarterly "realization team" sessions with the top 250 leaders to make certain that they understood and embraced strategic priorities. Equally important, these sessions were designed to collectively engage the organization in ongoing conversations that connect *why* the enterprise exists, *what* the goals are for the bank and each teammate, and *how* to execute against these goals. Through this process, purpose and performance were inextricably linked in a very concrete way. It also helped guide decision making and set guardrails for acceptable behavior.

Beyond the realization teams, SunTrust also implemented quarterly town halls for every business segment and function, ensuring full company alignment to the strategic priorities and allowing two-way interaction on both shared and specific objectives.

UPS: Engage others to keep "Eyes on the Enterprise." David Abney, CEO of UPS, formalized the process of communicating and aligning the company's strategic intent with everyone in the organization through strategy maps and a game.

In 2014, UPS surveyed managers to see what they knew about the UPS strategy and how connected they felt to it. The results were troubling because the data suggested their knowledge was low. But the good news was that managers and supervisors felt accountable and had a strong sense of responsibility to understand the strategy and communicate it to their teams. They wanted to learn more about where the company was headed, and they wanted to learn it by working together, face-to-face, with their peers and partners. UPS's solution was to create a strategy map that illustrated the key elements of the strategy, and a collaborative game experience called "Eyes on the Enterprise" that put UPSers together to learn the strategy by assuming the role of decision makers. By making choices about which strategic areas require people, time, and investment, and then debriefing the implications of those choices, the players came away with a richer, more grounded, and more actionable knowledge of what the strategy means to customers, the company, and to themselves.

The UPS leadership team defined the strategic purpose, then worked with the communications group to design visual maps as discussion starters (see Table 3.1 for an example). In the map's images and explanations, the UPS vision and strategy are brought to life. According to Abney, the strategy map discussions helped the employees "navigate toward their destination" and generate "boundless opportunities to learn, share, and live the strategy." The process helped employees at all levels understand how they contribute to the strategy, own it, and invest in it.

"Eyes on the Enterprise" is a cascading process, and one that UPS views as absolutely necessary as it expands globally. Jim Barber, president of UPS International, sees the power of the strategic map discussions in driving alignment through every level of the team. "We are giving regional managers today at UPS actually more insights into the business than we gave the management committee ten to fifteen years ago," Barber says. "So we're stretching that rubber band a bit."

The process engages managers in conversations with their direct reports to help them better understand, own, and demonstrate the strategy in their daily actions and decisions. And although the tool of strategy maps has been around for some time, it's core to vertical alignment at UPS. The maps help people to not only learn the strategy but also find themselves and the work they do represented in it. In effect, it helps them to operationalize the strategy and own it.

Microsoft: Create a multilevel dialogue. Satya Nadella's priorities for alignment led to relentlessly communicating a clear, concise, repeatable connection between Microsoft's mission, strategy, ambitions, leadership principles, and culture (see Figure 3.1).

On his first day as CEO, Nadella sent an email to employees that read in part, "Make no mistake, we are headed for greater places—as technology evolves and we evolve with and ahead of it. Our job is to ensure that Microsoft thrives in a mobile and cloud-first world. . . . As we look forward, we must zero in on what Microsoft can uniquely contribute to the world. The opportunity ahead will require us to reimagine

TABLE 3.1 UPS Strategy Mapping

Key Elements of the Map	Description	Discover and Discuss
VISION	Connecting a global community through intelligent logistics networks helps to inspire engagement in the company and ideals.	What does the vision statement say about UPS's future direction?
VALUE STACK	(a) sophisticated high-value solutions, (b) our broad portfolio of products and capabilities, (c) our efficient global network, and (d) delivered by expert people and partners	What is the value stack? How does each layer help differentiate UPS? Think about what your local customers value from UPS. How do you and your team help deliver that value? How can you increase it?
ENTERPRISE STRATEGY	(a) create value for customers (shippers and receivers), (b) transform to strengthen its leadership position, and (c) invest to accelerate and grow	Describe how your team supports UPS's strategy.
KEY CAPABILITY AREAS FOR INVESTMENT	(a) customer solutions, (b) targeted industries, (c) global markets/trade, (d) the everything-economy, and (e) integrated technologies	Why do you think the Five Strategic Area Medallions at the top of the map are key investment areas of the enterprise strategy?
ONE UPS	(1) Operate with energy, agility, and customer centricity to make it easier for more customers to use UPS's products and solutions, (2) Evaluate every aspect of the business and collaborate across units and functions to reduce organizational friction, (3) Offer and develop innovative ideas to help ease customer pain points, (4) Support our Marketing, Sales, and Solutions teams as they position the right products and services for our customer, (5) Solve problems and work together to provide seamless, customer-centric experiences.	How can we work together across the enterprise to best present One UPS to our customers? Why is this so important?
VALUES	Our granite foundation of enduring beliefs that define UPS people, the company, and our brand.	How do our values help UPS people deliver an exceptional customer experience?
CREATING THE FUTURE:	Empowering, innovating, and growing together	How does "empowering together" enable customers to view UPS as a trusted advisor? How can we better empower those we lead? What enhancements has "Innovating Together" created for today's shippers and receivers? On a local level, how can we better innovate to meet the future needs of our customers? Besides adding customers, and growing revenue and volume, what does "Growing Together" mean to us?

Source: United Parcel Service of America, Inc. Reprinted with permission.

a lot of what we have done in the past for a mobile and cloud-first world, and do new things."[14] Nadella worked with his senior leadership team to create tighter focus, alignment, and direction.

By all accounts, a key inflection point was when the senior leaders were standing together at their global summit, the entire team came out on stage to kick off a new era of integrated leadership. Hogan reflected on the significance. "I can't tell you how much positive feedback we've gotten on that," she explains. "It was five minutes, but it was symbolic, and I think it goes to this alignment point. People want to see that the leadership team is aligned. They're in it together. And if you can create that, it can be a huge accelerator."

To keep the message consistent and flowing, Nadella built a steady cadence of meetings and forums to test and reinforce alignment. Nadella established a standing meeting with his team every Friday, with one objective—to reinforce alignment on the three ambitions at the time: build the intelligent cloud platform, create more personal computing, and reinvent productivity and business processes. Not only does Nadella's team meet every Friday, but each of those leaders met with their respective

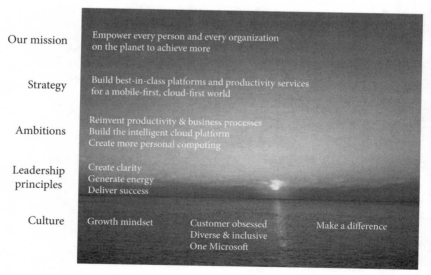

Our mission	Empower every person and every organization on the planet to achieve more
Strategy	Build best-in-class platforms and productivity services for a mobile-first, cloud-first world
Ambitions	Reinvent productivity & business processes Build the intelligent cloud platform Create more personal computing
Leadership principles	Create clarity Generate energy Deliver success
Culture	Growth mindset Customer obsessed Make a difference Diverse & inclusive One Microsoft

FIGURE 3.1 Microsoft Alignment
Source: Microsoft Corporation. Reprinted with permission.

groups each week as well. These cascading meetings continued further into the Microsoft organization over and over (and over).

While such meeting structures are not particularly unique, what's different at Microsoft is their steady cadence. Leaders never go more than a week without the organization iterating on points that are most critical.

These meetings are also a way to surface issues upward, and bring information to the senior leadership team. It's Microsoft, so Nadella uses the company's social media platform to keep the conversation going. He has a monthly, in-person, live Q&A that also utilizes Yammer (Microsoft's enterprise social networking platform), open to all employees regardless of geography. They ask everything from deep questions on strategy to technical questions on products.

Hogan says the sessions help drive alignment because "everyone's voice matters, and anyone can ask a question." She believes the payoff has been clear. "Satya did a great job creating clarity around our focus on personal computing, on the cloud and productivity, and again that clarity then allows people to drive alignment around it."

Do people in your organization understand how their work aligns with your strategic intent? These examples illustrate just a few ways to engage employees cognitively and emotionally to improve alignment. In all cases, the senior leadership teams need to define the strategic intent, engage each level of managers to translate and operationalize the mission, and create opportunities for dialogue all the way to the front lines. How you do this must fit your organization's challenges, culture, and capabilities. But we're confident these examples give you some good ideas.

RAISE SHARED EXPECTATIONS

As much as clarifying strategic intent is critical for achieving alignment, it is only the first step. There's more to the process. The companies we've worked with emphasize that you need to bring the strategic intent to life, give it energy, and build collective ambition and aspiration. The key is to convert energy from the top leadership to the rest of the organization through shared expectations for excellence.

"It's all about managing expectations," as one executive put it. Is everyone aiming high? Check yourself on the following questions:

- How do we establish and reinforce shared expectations for high performance throughout our organization?
- Which values, behaviors, and norms of excellence are embedded in our culture?
- In what ways does our culture encourage employees to challenge one another and bring forth new ideas?

Aim High: What's Possible and What's Necessary?

The uncomfortable reality is that to achieve executional excellence, senior leaders frequently need to recalibrate expectations about performance. It's somewhat surprising how often individuals and entire organizations have become content to just lumber along. But it's not uncommon. Leaders need to continually renew their commitments to excellence themselves and demonstrate that commitment to others.

Shared expectations for high performance do two key things. First, they raise our ambitions for the organization, lifting a sense of what's possible—what's anticipated in the future. Second, they ground the organization by reflecting what's required or necessary—the normative behaviors, values, and standards of excellence to which we must adhere. We found these fundamentals drove key initiatives in the companies we profile here, but each followed a different path. As you'll see in the following examples, Vail Resorts, Microsoft, and SunTrust applied different practices to follow the "aim high" principle.[15]

Vail Resorts: Challenge old ways of thinking. For many years, Vail Resorts enjoyed a cadre of dedicated, passionate employees in a business that was somewhat of a cottage industry. Many were avid skiers, rose through the ranks, and spent their entire careers in the ski business. They knew the industry, they knew the company, and they revered its culture.

Unfortunately, they didn't know how to run a world-class corporation—nor did they have the will to make it happen. Early on, Katz realized that success at Vail required a major transformation, raising the bar on performance expectations; he asked his team to function as a "world class public company." Employees did not reject the idea—many simply didn't see it. At least not at first.

To create a step change in performance expectations, Katz had to challenge Vail's norms of polite engagement, replacing it with frank feedback and candid debate on why, what, and how the organization would operate differently. He had to create new rules of engagement, spelling out expectations for excellence in concrete terms to drive performance.

Some executives didn't want the change. Others were not capable of leading it. Within a couple of years, most of Katz's original team had moved on. But the leaders who remained, along with new members of the Vail executive team, converged to recast the organization.

Someone once told us, "To transform an organization you either have to change the people . . . or change the people." The reality of achieving executional excellence is that some leaders like old, habitual ways of doing things, and they either won't change—or can't.

If members of your leadership team aren't willing to accept and exemplify high performance expectations, you have to make the tough call and make changes on your team.

Microsoft: Learn to perfect your "swing." Like Katz, Nadella had high expectations for his senior leadership team, asking them to be "all in" as they drove "clarity, alignment, and intensity all their work."[16] More important, several Microsoft leaders told us, Nadella set a personal example.

Fortunately, higher expectations were a welcome change for the Microsoft team. In fact, employees had been waiting for them—really wanted them. Scott Guthrie, executive VP of the Cloud and Enterprise Group, explained, "There was sort of an existential angst inside the company of are we past our prime? Can we compete? We've got a lot of good people, a lot of type A people, and once you get them energized and focused and raring to go, we were able to leverage that and really apply that talent in some amazing ways."

Nadella likened Microsoft's challenge to that of a high-performing rowing team working in perfect synchronization. "Many crews, even winning crews, never really find it," Nadella explained. "Others find it but can't sustain it. It's called 'swing.' It only happens when all eight oarsmen are rowing in such perfect unison that no single action by any one is out of synch with those of all the others. . . . Poetry, that's what a good swing looks like. As a company, as a leadership team, as individuals, that is our goal—to find our swing."

Challenging high commitment and connecting the vision, tone, and actions at the top with a ready and willing team allowed Microsoft to not only raise their aspirations but also begin performing at a higher level.

Is High Performance Embedded in Your Culture?

Although there are overt steps that leaders can take to raise and reinforce shared performance expectations, the strongest and most enduring lever is to embed it in the culture. Unfortunately, that isn't so simple.

In the context of execution, Larry Bossidy, former CEO of Honeywell, argued for demystifying the word *culture*. "Stripped to its essentials, an organization's culture is the sum of its shared values, beliefs, and norms of behavior."[17] As the foundation of the organization's culture, shared expectations serve both as points of normative behavior and guardrails for acceptable action.

In his book, *Who Says Elephants Can't Dance*, Lou Gerstner describes why execution needs to be embedded in the culture.

> I came to see, in my time at IBM, that culture isn't just one aspect of the game—
> it is the game. In the end, an organization is nothing more than the collective
> capacity of its people to create value. Vision, strategy, marketing, financial man-
> agement—and management system, in fact—can set you on the right path and
> can carry you for a while. But no enterprise—whether in business, government,
> education, health care or any area of human endeavor—will succeed over the
> long haul if those elements aren't part of its DNA.[18]

So how do you embed "aim high" in your organization's culture? There is no one way to do it, but we can learn from how some companies are striving to make it part of their DNA.

Marriott: Do unto others. . . . When Arne Sorenson talks about the requirements of execution at Marriott, and the power of alignment, he begins with a focus on culture. As he put it, "When we think about execution, we think about culture. Because without culture, the execution might be done by rote, but it's not going to be done with the kind of pride that it must be done." Marriott associates take pride in high levels of customer service—a reflection of how they themselves are treated, leadership performance expectations, and the company's business model. As Sorenson put it, "The culture is . . . 'Take care of the associate, and the associate will take care of the guest, and the guest will come back again and again.'" As simple as the concept seems, it is the foundation of Marriott's culture. "In this day and age, it sounds a little trite maybe or almost a little soft and squishy. It's really not. It's about how do you stay focused on building opportunity for folks . . . and hold them on performance by all means."

The notion of an "employee-customer-profit chain" has been around for some time, and many organizations have tried to embed it in their culture. Few have succeeded.[19] The simple idea that satisfied employees create satisfied customers is intuitive and laudable, but the inevitable push and shove of business realities often crowds out its philosophical roots.

How does Marriott do it?

CHRO David Rodriguez explains it this way: "An important ingredient to Marriott's secret sauce is creating a caring and engaging work environment that inspires associates to deliver exceptional customer experiences. They come to see even the smallest of tasks as significant components to the company's vision to be the world's favorite travel company."

Karl Fischer, chief HR officer for the Americas, reinforces the importance of caring about the whole person so that they bring their whole selves to the customer experience. He explains, "Between 85 and 90 percent of the work force is being paid by the hour to do jobs that are in some cases routine . . . and so the first job is to really engage them because they're the front line with all of your guests."

Marriott's approach is to show they care about employees twenty-four hours a day. Supervisors are expected to go beyond first names to know their team members' families, dreams, and concerns. "You engage the whole person, not just the eight hours that they hang out with you," Fischer said. "We try really hard to care about the whole person, and I think that's a different kind of experience when they come to Marriott than they've had with other employers."

According to Sorenson, the payoff is that employees take ownership. They believe "'I am the face of Marriott,'" he explained. "'I may be a housekeeper who only has fifteen rooms on this floor, but I'm proud of what I accomplish for Marriott. I'm proud to work for this company, and I'm going to take my work seriously.'"

When culture is the foundation for alignment, it can be a potent element of execution. But it doesn't happen overnight. Fischer joked, "Companies call us and say, 'Can you consult with us or teach us how to create a culture like yours,' and we say, 'Do you have 70 years?'"

The lesson from Marriott? Model your high standards for the customer experience in how you treat your team. When that's how you do business, it takes root and becomes your culture.

Microsoft: Connect behavior to business outcomes. Nadella also knew Microsoft's culture had to change in order to reinvigorate a spirit of excellence. His approach to change was very deliberate and thoughtful, first engaging employees through surveys and roundtables to determine what culture elements to keep and where to evolve. "There's a lot about Microsoft's culture and our heritage that we're proud of, that we never want to change." Hogan explained. "But in our new world, how do we need to evolve?"

Nadella's leadership team took the feedback seriously, analyzing it through a three-day executive offsite. They arrived at five key cultural attributes to take Microsoft forward: growth mindset, customer obsessed, diverse and inclusive, One Microsoft, and make a difference. These five were derived from, and focused on, Microsoft's strategic intent. That focus on strategic intent is a linchpin that may help ensure its success. As Bossidy and Charan observed, "Most efforts at culture change fail because they are not linked to improving the business's outcomes."[20] To ensure follow-through, Nadella formed a "culture cabinet" to hold the leadership team accountable for results. There is a constant reminder at Microsoft that these changes are a foundation for achieving greater capability.

Let's take this one step further. Microsoft's concept of a growth mindset connects to its bold ambitions and is rooted in Carol Dwek's work that distinguishes growth versus fixed mindsets. "If you take two people, one of them is a learn-it-all and the other one is a know-it-all, the learn-it-all will always trump the know-it-all in the long run, even if they start with less innate capability," Nadella explained. "A growth mindset emphasizes execution as learning, asking not telling, not being afraid to make mistakes but recognizing that learning fast requires some risk. It embraces the idea of the uncertainty and ambiguity, giving people a foundation for resilience in the face of change."[21]

Because many at Microsoft were eager for—looking for—an aligned team and culture change, Nadella's efforts took root and inspired higher expectations for the company. And they built momentum and behavioral expectations to see it through.

UPS: Trust delivers. Recall from Chapter 1 that when Jim Casey and Claude Ryan started UPS, their original idea was to create a small messenger service with just a few people delivering messages in San Francisco. They convinced a few customers to trust that they would get the job done reliably—to "deliver" on their promise. The company grew, and some would say UPS was the original platform company. Buyers and sellers (shippers and receivers) had confidence—and trust—that UPS would help them complete their business transactions.

And to this day, UPS executives insist that trust is the foundation of their business model. It is more than just core to their culture; it is the heart of their value proposition. Violate trust and the company falters. CEO David Abney put it this way: "I don't think you can ever compromise on your values. Any short-term gain comes at the risk of long-term reputational harm."[22] Chief Human Resources Officer Teri McClure added, "We have to maintain that level of trust because we're stewards on behalf of our customers of their valuable goods."

The UPS culture is based on shared expectations for performance built on discipline, accountability, and respect for others. The founding principles established by Jim Casey more than one hundred years ago continue to guide the company today. "Literally we start off every meeting with a policy book discussion," McClure said. From David Abney team on down, the UPS policy book is a constant reminder of their heritage, and the company's culture and founding principles are frequently discussed in daily meetings with employees.

As UPS has grown, its values-based model has been critical to the company's high performance. "We hire a lot of people," McClure said. "People who gravitate toward the culture will feel comfortable here. People who don't gravitate toward the culture ultimately won't enjoy working in this environment."

The company's commitment to trust and execution translates to global expansion decisions, including countries where they choose to operate. Countries that share UPS's high service standards get more investment than those that don't. They've learned this the hard way at times, but UPS is up front with prospective partners that doing business with them hinges on alignment around shared values and expectations. As Jim Barber put it, "You're bringing human beings and commerce together in a very unique way, and in the middle is this word 'trust.' In a business like ours that works on trust, you just don't go until the governance model's right. . . ."

The bottom line: UPS aims high in their expectations for trust—inside and outside the company. It's the foundation of their pact with customers, the privilege of working on their team and of decisions about where they do business. It's part of their DNA.

The UPS story, as well as that of Marriott and Microsoft, show there is more than one way to instill shared expectations for performance into a culture. And as we've seen, it takes work to make "aim high" central to your business.

ENSURE MUTUAL ACCOUNTABILITY FOR RESULTS

If the first two steps toward better alignment are to create a clear strategic intent and build shared expectations for high performance, the third step is to close the loop through a system of mutual accountability.

perfunctory. Katz and his team take ownership for their performance and share clear, candid feedback with each other. In our experience, that's what sets Vail apart and is an important part of what they've learned in their execution journey.

Is Accountability Implicit?

As much as the formal elements of performance management can facilitate shared accountability and alignment, we offer one word of caution. Traditional performance systems can backfire if they lead to fear, unhealthy competition, or a sense of control and micromanagement. They are only one piece of the puzzle.

The vast majority of CEOs we've talked to say shared accountability needs to be internalized and implicit to the character of leadership. As one executive told us, "It's about holding *yourself* accountable, as well as holding your people accountable. Ultimately shared accountability comes down to the personal stake individuals have in the business."

Marriott: Beyond scorecards. Marriott works to balance the formality of metrics with the informality of personal touch. On the metrics side of things, Marriott has its version of the balanced scorecard that focuses on three stakeholder priorities: the guest, the associate, and the hotel owner and the company shareholder (financial performance).[24] In the back of the house of most Marriotts, there's some sort of scoreboard. Everyone knows it, and everyone in one form or fashion is working to hit the shared goals and objectives that typically relate to those three priorities.

Getting the balance right is a challenge, and one that Marriott takes seriously. Fischer put it this way: "We certainly do attempt to pull it through in a performance appraisal, through our bonus . . . what we incent people around, but there's this general understanding that there are multiple stakeholders that play in those three general buckets, and our job as leaders is to balance them to try to create win-win-win. Three wins."

Just as no world-class athlete would want to play a sport without keeping score, metrics help world-class organizations know how well they're doing. "You're keeping score, and you want to win," says Fischer. "Most human beings want to win. So you play with that a little bit. So, you know, how you keep score or accountability is important."

But Fischer emphasized that these scorecards are merely tools for reinforcing shared accountability and managing the business, not rules that program behavior. "So when I think about what keeps them [associates] focused, it's everyone just from a cultural perspective knows that we as a company are trying to balance creating great experiences for the guests, driving financial performance for our shareholders, many of which are employees, and also having as engaged a work force as possible."

Marriott is fervently focused on being an engagement leader. For them, merely doing better than last year or better than the industry norm is not good enough. They dig deeper, driving leadership accountability to a more granular level.

Vail Resorts: Tough love. As much as Vail has gotten lift from formalizing performance management to make accountability explicit, the system is not a substitute for personal leadership. Effective leaders are accountable for engaging in candid conversations with their teams. CEO Katz recognizes that sometimes he needs to have difficult conversations with people who love the business but need a dose of reality. "In our company, because we have so much positive passion and emotion around our sport, we self-select people who are here for a very aspirational and higher minded purpose. . . . [But] on accountability, 99 times out of 100 it's because you don't have the tough conversation with somebody or make the tough decision. That is what accountability is."

Does he risk damaging or demoralizing his organization with brutal facts? It's all in the delivery, and a risk worth taking. "I think one of the biggest areas of misalignment in our company is thinking that I am helping someone by making them feel good when that is not constructive for the company, for them, or for the people who work for them."

Katz believes in his leaders, expects more from his leaders, and is getting more from his leaders. And he expects them to pass that on. He puts it this way to his team: "If you are a leader here, and you've got direct reports, then you better be good at your job or those direct reports are not going to be doing their job. So we need to hold you accountable to hold them accountable, too." Accountability—or lack thereof—can be contagious. The benefits of his approach are paying off. By making accountability an implicit aspect of his leadership team, Katz has elevated shared expectations and engendered personal accountability into Vail's culture.[25]

As with the other examples we have shared, this is not a cookie cutter deal. There's more than one way to approach accountability. From Marriott, we learned to balance performance that benefits guests, associates, and stockholders. From Vail, we learned to have ongoing, frank, and candid (even confrontational) discussions to prevent superficial alignment. And from SunTrust, we learned the value of full transparency, with leaders holding one other—and themselves—mutually accountable. These examples show the diversity of approaches that can prove useful, and while they reinforce the same principles, they also make clear the importance of choosing processes and solutions that work for your organization.

WHERE DO YOU STAND?

If you see yourself and your organization in some of these stories and anecdotes, good. That helps ground your reflection in concrete experience and channel your attention about what you need to do next. In some cases, you may be saying, "Yep, we're doing that" or maybe you're out in front—ahead of the companies we've mentioned. In other places, you may have this sinking feeling, forced to acknowledge that while you should be doing some of this, you're not. Or it's not working (well enough). You're in good company—as we've said repeatedly, executives in some excellent organizations have the same twin response to our questions: Yes, it's critical, and no, we're not there yet.

But when it comes to improving execution, alignment is a great place to start. As we said at the beginning of the chapter, alignment is an imperative. Not only do many CEOs see alignment as the most important enabler of execution, but it's also the first to be addressed because so much else hinges on it.

The challenge is real, and the threshold is high. Some CEOs, such as Terex's John Garrison, argue that 100 percent alignment needs to be the goal. Given his West Point roots, Garrison's obsession with execution may be self-evident. But his premise for 100 percent alignment is based on simple math. If there are even small gaps between the executives, those gaps get multiplied and compounded as you extend throughout the hierarchy. Makes sense. What may begin as incidental differences lead to greater confusion further into the organization. Garrison's leadership philosophy has become a corporate mantra. He ends all his strategy alignment meetings with the following question to be answered by each executive leadership team member: "Are you 100 percent committed to the strategy and 100% committed to your peers in executing our strategy?" In order to achieve this lofty 100 percent goal, he applies many of the principles and practices we've prescribed in this chapter.

Although we agree that 100 percent alignment is the ultimate goal, our experience tells us that the goal is never fully achieved and the job is never fully done. Despite its criticality, alignment is not a final destination, and you are never really quite there. It is either getting better or worse, but it is never complete. It's not a steady state. Organizations are too dynamic.

So what can you do about it? Step one is to define your current state. Where does your organization stand? Take a few minutes to evaluate yourself on the following checklist (Table 3.2)—give yourself and your organization a rating on a 1–5 scale, with 1 being unacceptable and 5 being exceptional.

Is one of the categories stronger or weaker than the others? Ask others on your team as well. Compare your responses. We've found two issues that come up when executives do these kinds of ratings. The first is that there are typically stronger or weaker areas, suggesting some problem areas where scores are lower. But there is an equally important issue—executives within the same team often give different ratings, sometimes markedly so. They see the issues and the organization differently. These are important areas for discussion as well. It's the difference between looking at the average rating, versus looking at the standard deviation. When it comes to alignment, both are important.

TABLE 3.2 Alignment Checklist

ALIGNMENT CHECKLIST	
Strategic Intent	1. Our strategy is clearly understood and supported by all managers.
	2. We have clear prioritized goals that our leaders regularly communicate throughout the enterprise.
	3. Our executive team models all the behaviors necessary to translate our strategy into performance.
Shared Expectations	4. Norms and expectations for high performance are shared throughout the organization.
	5. Our culture is defined by values, behaviors, and expectations of excellence.
	6. Our culture encourages employees to challenge and bring forth new ideas to peers and managers.
Accountability	7. Managers are held accountable for achieving results and actions that support our strategy.
	8. Rewards are connected to both individual and team performance.
	9. Individuals hold themselves accountable for results and execution of strategy across the entire enterprise.

© Scott A. Snell and Kenneth J. Carrig

After you've gone through this checklist, there are some signs of progress to look for. You'll likely see fewer of the symptoms we talked about at the beginning of the chapter: (1) getting diverted and sidetracked, (2) focusing on too many things leading to resource dispersion and firefights, and (3) flagging employee engagement, frustration, and decline.

Acting with Clarity and Continuity

Beyond that, you'll likely see executives and employees throughout the organization operating with more clarity and focus. Like there's more oxygen in the room—their eyes may even clear. Particularly during periods of disruption and change, they'll have more resilience to stay the course because that course is better defined *with* them, has more meaning and purpose, and they know their roles. Not only is the strategic intent clearer, the organization's identity is likely to be sharper. You'll see it first in the executive team interactions and collaboration, but our experience is that it can quickly energize the rank and file.

Engaging and Working in Harmony

Watch for more people working in harmony (if not unison). Harmony has two meanings here. First, there's the Zen-like quality of harmony—less discord, disagreement, and conflict. Nice. This will likely show up in morale and engagement surveys. It may even have a quick effect on other metrics like absenteeism and turnover. But also look for harmony in the sense that one player complements and enriches the other. This isn't just a passive form of support—you will likely see them pushing one another toward excellence, getting more from them. You may see evidence of knowledge sharing and voluntary prosocial behavior (aka helping one another), and mutual learning.

Getting Out In Front

An outgrowth of alignment is initiative. Vail's Rob Katz argues that real alignment enables his leaders to "get out front" to take initiative on behalf of the organization. This is not possible without alignment, and in a rapidly evolving environment the organization would not succeed if managers waited to be told what to do. We would emphasize that, done well, alignment empowers employees at all levels to do the right thing. It speeds and improves the quality of decision making and frees managers to work on more strategic things—employees make the right call on day-to-day and other matters. Alignment in this sense goes beyond a shared understanding and/or commitment, and includes some degree of discretion that empowers people with the latitude to execute within their roles. If execution is viewed only as a top-down initiative, the organization will miss contemporaneous opportunities that drive performance excellence from the bottom up. However, this is only possible because of alignment and accountability.

Capability Lifts Up

Begin to look for more organizational capability and lift in performance. With better alignment, you'll witness the release of energy that can build momentum and boost capability and internal performance. Look for changes in more proximate metrics like project management (on time, on budget), customer service and engagement scores, expense reductions, and the achievement of most critical operational objectives.

Be careful to keep focused on those elements that are most controllable. It would perhaps be unrealistic to expect significant changes in lagging indicators such as profitability, market share, and the like. More useful is to look at internal metrics such as time, quality, and costs.

External Validation

Finally, external stakeholders may notice as well. In addition to customers, changes in alignment are observable, even palpable, to external partners, suppliers, board members, and others. That's gratifying of course, but the effect is to reinforce improvement and amplify progress. That's not just a nice thing, it's a further catalyst for change.

(Many, many) years ago, when Ken was the head of HR at Continental Airlines, he was a key player in CEO Gordon Bethune's team to take the company from *Worst to First*.[26] Their "Go Forward Plan" created alignment in the entire organization, focusing first on taking care of customers, being safe, and flying on time. The turnaround at Continental was remarkably fast, and customers noticed immediately, even before the transformation was complete. When customers gave employees compliments, they beamed with pride, sometimes even tearing up for what they were achieving together. That external validation helped them calibrate their performance, and it galvanized alignment and accelerated the change.

WHAT NEXT? BUILDING THE TEAM: TALENT AND ABILITY

Throughout this chapter, we've explained the importance of establishing strategic intent, creating "aim high" expectations, and ensuring shared accountability. All are key to alignment and will make a difference in your organization's ability to execute. But we also need to tackle the other elements of our model: Ability, Architecture, and Agility.

In the next chapter, we cover the Ability element of the 4A framework. We delve into leadership explicitly and address how organizations are building effective leadership teams, ensuring a pipeline of key talent, and improving collaborative capability across the enterprise.

4 ABILITY

The Power of Talent

WHEN SATYA NADELLA was promoted to CEO of Microsoft, he knew that the company's future depended on developing new capabilities and new ways of working in a mobile- and cloud-first world of computing. The importance of talent and human capital had always been central to Microsoft's success, but Nadella's task was to build a leadership team that could reconfigure Microsoft and realign its talent pool around a culture of innovation, to take the company into new markets, with new services, and new technologies. Strategic execution means not only delivering on today's priorities, but also building the capacity to invent the future. In that regard, Nadella believed that nothing was more important than talent. How would Microsoft identify, acquire, develop, and deploy that talent going forward?[1]

Arne Sorenson viewed Marriott's challenge as somewhat different but no less transformative, and equally rooted in culture. In its acquisition of Starwood, there were literally hundreds of thousands of employees, managers, and executives who needed to come together under the Marriott marquee to take the company forward. How would Sorenson help these former competitors, with arguably very different cultures and business practices, build an organization that was even better together than they were apart? This would mean uniting legions of managers and employees, not just in the technical aspects of their work, but in their behavior toward guests and how they ran their hotels. Sorenson saw the challenge not simply as implementing an integration plan. It involved learning from one another, engaging the entire work force, to build a better organization.

Like Microsoft and Marriott, David Abney's team at UPS faced a challenge of ability, albeit a unique one among these peers. UPS knew that implementing its growth strategy in emerging markets meant rethinking some of its time-honored approaches to management. Its proud tradition of growing managers from within would be tested as the company pursued opportunities in new regions. How could they find local partners and build a pool of managerial talent that was capable and accountable in very different environments around the world? Where practices and work standards, values and ethics, were so dramatically different, how could UPS transport its time-honored approach? Executing its strategy depended on it.

Each of these stories shows the importance of "ability" writ large in executing strategy—the importance of leadership, talent, culture, and collaborative capability. In this chapter, we address the somewhat obvious point that organizational performance depends on assembling, developing, and deploying a talented group of leaders, managers, and employees.

That fact alone may not have evaded you. We hope. However, the growing strategic importance of human capital may be more surprising than you currently reckon. Research evidence is clear that the economic value of most organizations has shifted in a lopsided way from tangible assets, such as plant and equipment, to intangible assets, including human capital. An annual study by Ocean Tomo reported the portion of corporate market value attributable to intangible assets has grown from 17 percent in 1975 to a staggering 87 percent in 2015.[2] See the graphic trend in Figure 4.1 below.

Are companies shifting to take advantage, or at least keep up with these trends? The potential payoff is substantial. A recent study by the Drucker Institute found that fifty companies with the largest five-year gains in effectiveness also had the biggest increases in employee development and engagement. Perhaps not surprisingly, companies suffering the

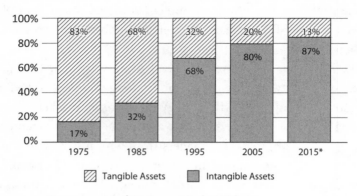

FIGURE 4.1 Components of S&P 500 Market Value
Source: Annual Study of Intangible Asset Market Value from Ocean Tomo, LLC, 2015. Reprinted with permission.

largest decreases in effectiveness also were off the most in employee development. Related research by Bersen/Deloitte backs this up; companies with an integrated talent strategy outperform their peers, generating more than twice the revenue per employee, 40 percent lower turnover rates, and 38 percent higher levels of employee engagement than their peers. However, it is startling to note that only a measly 7 percent of companies in that study had an integrated talent system (defined as a top-down-led program for leadership development, succession, development of strategic competencies, and continuous and structured reviews of talent).[3]

People are an organization's greatest asset (there, we have promulgated the platitude). But the fact is that many organizations, in an effort to drive efficiencies, still work to diminish the role of people in the production equation, preferring to invest in technologies as a substitute for humans. There's nothing inherently wrong with that. Except, in the contemporary setting where knowledge and learning are vital for breakthrough performance, human capital is an underlying fundamental for strategy execution.

SYMPTOMS OF THE TALENT SYNDROME

Unfortunately, many organizations suffer from what we call the "talent syndrome"; a recurring pattern of symptoms that lead to decline. It has an all-too-familiar set of conditions: (1) the organization is chronically short of talent, especially in key positions, (2) the company does not make talent management a top priority, (3) senior leaders scramble to fill key jobs, and (4) the company cannot execute against its business opportunities.

Firms limit what's possible when they suffer from the talent syndrome. It's not that they don't have good strategies. It's that they don't have the human resources to seize market opportunities. They have good ideas, capital, and market potential. But they haven't made the investments—ahead of the curve—in critical human resources to drive growth and profitability.

Why do we refer to this as a *syndrome*? It's not just a euphemism—a syndrome is a debilitating pattern of symptoms, recurring and consistently associated with one another, emanating from a deeper underlying cause. When we ask managers if they recognize symptoms of the talent syndrome in their own organizations, they often say yes. When we ask why, they scratch their heads. Let's consider the symptoms and see if you recognize any in your own organization. That can serve as a starting point for side stepping this major execution trap.

Symptom #1: Are You Frozen By Indecision?

The truth is that the future is often uncertain. One executive recently said in frustration "How do we prepare the organization for a future that is unclear—and keeps changing?!" He works in an industry undergoing rapid reinvention and disruption, so much disruption that it's nearly impossible to predict where it is going. He's not alone. Managers routinely tell us that it is difficult to make strategic investments in talent because the future is unknown, if not unknowable. Even some of the unknowns are unknown.

Although we sympathize with the situation, the response need not be to do nothing. As a matter of fact, continuous learning and development of talent and leadership may be the best remedy for an uncertain future. We will discuss this more in Chapter 6 on Agility. In his book *Learn or Die*, Ed Hess notes that, in dynamic environments, excellence and innovation require constant learning as an individual and as part of a learning organization. In short, your ability to learn is you best defense against an uncertain future.[4]

Symptom #2: Do You Default to Short-Termism?

Hockey legend Wayne Gretzky used to say, "A good hockey player skates to where the puck is; but a great hockey player skates to where the puck is going to be." We often ask managers whether their talent system is skating to where the puck is right now, or where it's going to be. Are they reacting to today's needs or investing for the future? They typically shake their heads and admit they skate to where the puck is right now. They are reactive. One manager once lamented, "We don't know what the puck we're doing."

Why? Well the point from above applies. Tomorrow is uncertain, so deal with what you can today. Fair enough, but that mindset can become cynical or insidious. "Tomorrow never comes." Or, "I'll worry about that tomorrow—I'm rewarded for delivering results today." These are common explanations that managers give for why their colleagues don't approach talent management in a strategic way. The problem is exacerbated when company profits are being squeezed.

In discussing short-termism, we'll scribble the following formula on a flip chart: $\pi = R - E$. (Profit equals revenues minus expenses). We'll ask managers, in the short term, how much can you increase revenues? "Not much," they say. So to boost profits in the short run, you're left with the expense part of the equation, right? What is your number one, most controllable expense? "People," they say.

Short-term emphasis on execution can lead us to focus on people as merely an expense. And so you're left in a quandary—you believe that people are your most important asset, but you manage them as if they are a cost to be reduced. Managers are smart, and they know their investment in people drives revenue and growth in the long run. But they have a hard time plugging that belief into the equation. And, with limited dollars to spend and limited time to deliver results, they'll regrettably make decisions that run counter to their better selves. They lament this situation, but admit that they often fail to muster a viable counterargument. In the urgency of execution, short-termism can lead to bad decisions about talent.

Symptom #3: Are You Spending Too Much Time Playing Defense?

A related problem is that sometimes managers will tell us that they are "too busy running the business" to spend so much time on talent. Many years ago, one manager we talked with brazenly eschewed the whole idea of needing a long-term view of talent. He was executing for today, and viewed headcount as a commodity that could be purchased as/when needed. "If I need engineers, I'll hire engineers," he said. But, this is a dangerous attitude. Contrast that with the CEO of a global energy company who chided his team for being too reactionary when it came to human capital. He said, "We need to think of talent management not as filling jobs but as creating strategic capability for tomorrow."

This CEO had it right and the other manager had it wrong: In our experience, hiring only when things become urgent and otherwise disregarding your talent pipeline keeps everyone playing defense, reacting rather than getting out front to proactively craft a talent strategy. If talent management is de facto relegated to filling jobs, the organization will ultimately fall short in execution.

The knee-jerk reaction to this situation might be to give HR more authority to create a robust and proactive (rather than reactive) approach to talent management. This has some merit in that the HR team can and should play a leadership role when it comes to talent. But line executives and the CEO must "own" the talent system. Indeed, Doug Ready and Jay Conger studied a number of top companies and found that the vitality of the talent management system depends on alignment and shared accountability with line executives (note the connection to our previous chapter). Particularly when the CEO personally leads the effort, the narrative within the organization is much different and the approach has more traction.[5]

WHAT CAN YOU DO?

If you recognize any of these symptoms in your organization, you're not alone. The talent syndrome is as widespread as it is debilitating. On top of the direct costs of poor performance, it's also leads to higher opportunity costs from forgone business prospects. That is why the Talent Syndrome is such a real threat to performance.

In the previous chapter, we noted that many CEOs believe alignment is the most important factor and the one to address first to improve execution capability. CEOs would also hasten to add, "Ability takes the longest to curate." It needs to be built up over time, and while you can make strategic external hires, execution excellence is more broadly rooted in the entire organization.

Our research shows that organizations can improve execution ability when they do three things:

- Focus on leadership, starting at the top and grounding the leaders' skill set in your strategy and cultural values.
- Establish a leadership and talent pipeline, especially in key jobs, and build talent capacity throughout your organization.
- Build collaborative capability internally and externally that acts as a talent multiplier.

In other words, the "ability" requirement of execution takes time, but with targeted investment you can build it up more swiftly. Addressing the challenge involves several related actions. Let's take a closer look at each one.

THERE'S NO SUBSTITUTE FOR LEADERSHIP

Especially in the context of strategic execution, leadership matters and can manifest in many different places in myriad different ways. In the previous chapter, we made a point to show how senior leaders must establish a clear strategic intent, build alignment horizontally and vertically, raise shared expectations of performance, and imbed accountability in the organization. But it goes beyond that. Leaders embody the strategy of the organization. They are stewards of its culture. Without good leaders, execution is unlikely. Check yourself on the following questions:

- In what ways do our leaders exhibit the breadth and depth of skills, competencies, and experience needed for breakthrough performance?
- Do we have the right mix of leaders who bring out the best in one another on behalf of the organization?

- Do our leaders inspire and empower others to achieve organizational goals?

Do Your Leaders Embody the Strategy?

Start at the top. If you don't have the right leaders to lead the company, it's hard to make up for it any other way. The CEO role is obviously both distinctive and valuable in the organization. In our experience, much is attributed to CEOs as they in some ways personify the organization, its strategy, and its culture. This may be an oversimplification, but it is most often the case. Both internally and externally, people look to the CEO as the genesis of strategy execution. And their visibility amplifies everything they do. We are not arguing for a "great wo/man" theory of leaders. In fact, the evidence is pretty clear that some of the best CEOs are very collaborative and humble, and let others share the limelight.[6] They enact several key functions with and through others. Let's look at Microsoft's Satya Nadella as an example.

Microsoft: The leader as role model. In many ways, Satya Nadella personifies the transformation taking hold at Microsoft. He obviously has had some big expectations foisted on him, and is inevitably compared to both founder Bill Gates and his predecessor, Steve Ballmer. And he has been expected to drive significant change to reinvigorate the company's leadership in a fiercely competitive industry.

Before choosing Nadella as CEO, Microsoft's board first looked inside and outside the company for the best candidates. The board was rumored to consider leaders such as Steven Elop (former Nokia CEO) and Alan Mulally (former Ford CEO). In the end, the search committee picked Nadella because he was uniquely qualified for the job and deemed to be a bright light for the company's future.

Recall in Chapter 2 we noted that Nadella rose rapidly through the company with key customer-facing, R&D, and technical solutions roles. His development path helped him forge key relationships and gain a perspective for both consumer and enterprise customers. He led some of Microsoft's most profitable and high-growth businesses and had shown the courage and insight to break from the company's characteristic proprietary approach and support open sourcing. He also championed innovative versions of products and services at a time when Microsoft was slow with updates. Perhaps most noteworthy, Nadella ran the Cloud Computing business in the months immediately preceding his promotion to CEO, giving him the gravitas to lead what would become a strategy heavily centered in cloud services. When he asked for big changes, he had the credibility to back it.

Many observe that Nadella reflects some of the attributes of his mentor, Bill Gates; his passion for learning and innovation, his deep technical skills and research acumen. He also reflects attributes of another mentor, Steve Ballmer, demonstrating great business acumen as well, positively impacting the diverse business units he led. And his track record showed strong interpersonal skills—Nadella built robust relationships inside and outside the organization. As one executive put it, "He's a consummate insider with an outsider's perspective." Especially important was his relationship with Microsoft's board of directors. In selecting Nadella as CEO, the board showed confidence that he had demonstrated ability to shift the organization's direction and guide it into areas others might not venture, given its legacy in traditional (desktop) software.

In a nutshell, Nadella embodies some of the most important aspects of Microsoft's strategy, combining their technical core, business vision, and a focus on employees and customers. "Satya is a proven leader with hard-core engineering skills, business vision, and the ability to bring people together," Bill Gates explained in an interview when Nadella was named CEO. "His vision for how technology will be used and experience around the world is exactly what Microsoft needs as the company enters its next chapter of expanded product innovation and growth."[7]

One more point about Nadella. His team regularly mentions how he models the behavior change that he expects from others. Microsoft has three primary leadership principles—create clarity, generate energy, and deliver success—and employees note that Nadella makes these principles a priority in everything he does. People see in him what he asks of them, and the effect is contagious. Kathleen Hogan sums it up this way: "It's what Satya tries to do, and therefore we're all trying to role model."

CEOs don't always need to come from the inside. Indeed some of the best are brought in from outside to shake things up. But, like Nadella, they need to have the personal credibility and influence to take the organization forward. Strategic execution depends on their building an energized organization with a clear vision and the capacity—rooted in the qualities of its people—to drive breakthrough performance.

Are You Playing the Best Team?

As important as the CEO is, the top management team are the ones who initiate the game plan and have responsibilities for/to others who will ultimately make strategy happen. They are that key point of translation from strategic intent to operational directives. From above and below, we continually hear that it's critical to get the team right. Yet it's often a challenge to get the right people in the right roles. There needs to be a balance across the players in terms of knowledge of the business, knowledge of their functions, and ability to collaborate across the team.

Legendary UCLA basketball coach John Wooden used to say, "I don't play my five best; I play my best five." Too many CEOs ascribe to a "best athlete" approach to their top teams, promoting high performers into senior roles both as a reward for achievement and an incentive for further contribution. In some cases, this creates an undeveloped "team of rivals" that breeds unhealthy competition and power plays among the most senior leaders. At a minimum, it can lead to those leaders developing fiefdoms, hoarding resources, and erecting silos. In addition to a lack of alignment, this creates dysfunction throughout the organization that impairs strategy execution. Better to find the right combination of leaders, even if this means not always promoting your stars. Ron Wallace, former president of UPS International, reinforced why, saying, "Nine times out of ten, teamwork trumps talent."[8]

In our experience, where companies go wrong is simply assigning people to teams or accepting the teams that exist and expecting them to be ready, willing, and able to collaborate. This false belief is that any group of people within the organization can be assembled into a team where the whole is greater than the sum of its parts.

We're not downplaying the importance of individual talent—it's crucial—but the collaborative effect is critical as well. Let's look at a couple of examples from SunTrust and Marriott, to illustrate these points and gain specific insights on how to groom the top team.

SunTrust: Start with the core players. Bill Rogers would fervently agree with Coach Wooden's advice about getting the best team in the game. When he became CEO of SunTrust, one of his first questions was "What and who do I need on my executive team?"

From a "what" standpoint, Rogers recognized that coming out of the financial crisis his executive team needed both deep vertical and broad horizontal competencies to compete and grow in the complex financial services environment. So he took several immediate actions to make that happen. He shifted a few of his most trusted direct reports into key leadership roles that were critical to the enterprise going forward. For example, he moved his then CFO, Mark Chancy, into a role leading the wholesale business, taking advantage of his deep financial acumen and experience. He promoted his treasurer to CFO. He moved his head of capital markets, Jerome Lienhard, to run the mortgage division.

Each of these moves was focused on critical business units, central to SunTrust's growth strategy. And Rogers had great confidence in these leaders, knowing the businesses would benefit from their deep functional expertise. Not coincidentally, these moves were also broadening roles for the leaders, which reinforced Rogers's emphasis on building an enterprise team who could deliver the whole bank. Moving functional leaders into P&L roles had the added benefit of combining perspectives that helped integrate line and staff priorities.

To round out his team, Rogers named a private wealth management leader to the CMO position, brought in a new CIO from the outside to strengthen SunTrust's use of information technology, and hired a new CHRO to reinforce the company's culture and people management. Finally, Rogers consolidated the previously segmented consumer businesses into one, and then recruited a new leader from an outside larger banking institution. In all cases, Rogers looked for top functional expertise and business acumen. But equally important, he sought true team players who would support and challenge each other on behalf of the bank and its customers.

What was the effect of all these moves? In Rogers's view, it created a tighter leadership team with deeper professional expertise, whose members would complement one another in taking the enterprise forward. He recognized that these "Ability" composition decisions were critical to SunTrust effectively executing its strategy in the short and long term. And he expected and rewarded cross-functional teamwork. The strategies worked: SunTrust's performance over that six-year window resulted in a significant improvement of its efficiency ratio (expense/revenue management) from 72 percent to 62 percent or nearly $726 million in savings while growing their market cap from $9.5 billion in 2011 to almost $27 billion in 2016.

How might you apply SunTrust's experience to your own organization? First, place teamwork at the top of your priorities within your C-suite. If it's lacking, address it. Don't hesitate to place some of your most trusted and most promising executives into new stretch roles. Second, build an effective support team around them and bring in others with complementary skills to balance out the team.

Leaders must be both discerning and decisive in putting the right people in the right roles to increase performance potential and take the company forward. One of the things we hear most often from CEOs is that they wish they had made personnel changes more quickly. While it is important to let individuals and the team grow and develop, if you see it's not working, make changes immediately. Execution depends on it.

Marriott: Know when to hold 'em. Sometimes you have to be smart enough not to mess with success. When Marriott acquired Starwood, one of the first orders of business was deciding who would take the combined company forward. Marriott already had a high-performing leadership team, and CHRO David Rodriguez was clear they were not going to risk destabilizing it by blindly following typical merger prescriptions. For example, Marriott did not place two executives in every leadership role for a period of time before deciding who would lead— a strategy that often contributes to internal conflict and poor merger performance. Marriott kept its leadership team intact, and selected only one of the Starwood senior leadership team members who, based on their assessment, brought unique incremental value to the combined company. This enabled an already cohesive and focused management team to get the newly combined company off to a strong start.

Marriott did bring over key executives from Starwood to add new roles to the team, including their head of loyalty programs. The Starwood Preferred Guest loyalty program was arguably the best in the industry, and one of the reasons that Marriott was initially interested in the acquisition. "That [move] was to showcase some of the reasons we did the deal," said Ty Breland, Marriott global head of talent and organizational capability. "They had some really great talent as it relates to loyalty and in the brand space . . . really brand-centric thinkers, they've acclimated really well to the company."

And there were many other roles for Starwood leaders, just one level down, in the thirty brands across five geographic segments. Three of those segments are now run by Starwood executives, and two by Marriott.

Sorenson said that, as CEO, he wanted to make the changes as quickly as possible. "For this deal to be successful, we need it to be for our shareholders, but we don't do that if it's not successful for our three principal communities: our associates, our guests, and our owners," he said. "We've always been associate focused, and we want them to feel good about the direction of the company."

Marriott's experience, while distinct from SunTrust's, shares a few common principles. First, at a strategic level, each CEO began with an assessment of the *organizational* capabilities needed to execute against the business's strategic intent. At SunTrust it was a turnaround; at Marriott it was a successful acquisition and integration with Starwood. Depending on that assessment, the CEO made two related decisions. First, what are the qualities that individual leaders need in each role? Technical/functional, business, and interpersonal skills. And are those leaders available in-house or is an external search needed? Related, and often more important, is how the leaders work together. Sometimes, the answer is simply to take the best-of-breed approach, the best individual athletes. But what we typically see, and these stories demonstrate, is that CEOs are biased toward teams versus individuals. This is where Ability meets Alignment in our 4A framework of strategic execution.

At SunTrust, Rogers ensured his C-suite had complementary talents not only to manage existing business but to transform the enterprise. And he placed equal weight on collaboration, ensuring each top leader was a team player. At Marriott, Sorenson made only minor tweaks to his high-performing senior leadership team. Rather than rock the boat, Marriott steadied it with a couple of strategic resources from Starwood.

The requirements of strategy are reflected in the key decisions about leadership team composition. Just as the CEO embodies the technical, business, and cultural imperatives of the strategy, so does the leadership team. Much is asked of them, and much is attributed to them.

INCREASE YOUR FIRM'S TALENT CAPACITY

As important as the CEO and leadership team are to strategy execution, we hear over and over—and we agree—that those who really make execution happen are deeper in the organization, the middle-level managers as well as rank-and-file employees. That's where real traction occurs. Lack of horsepower there stops the organization in its tracks. Unfortunately, as we noted at the outset of this chapter, too many organizations have an underpowered talent engine.

How effective is your organization's talent management system, building capacity in terms of both the stock and flow of skilled individuals in key roles? Check yourself against these questions:

- Have we identified "mission-critical" positions and staffed them with our top performers?
- Do we have a robust system for talent assessment to identify, develop, and retain high-quality employees?
- Are we investing in a talent pipeline to ensure a continual flow of "next generation" talent who are capable of leading us to the future?
- Do managers spend time coaching and developing employees and teams?

The experiences at Microsoft, SunTrust, Vail, Marriott, and UPS offer approaches you may consider for your company. Let's take a closer look.

Where Are Your Mission-Critical Positions?

Like any strategic asset, some people have a bigger impact on performance than others. But this impact is not necessarily associated with position in the hierarchy. The priority with regard to execution is generating more high performers, particularly in critical roles. An internal study at IBM pinpointed "focal jobs" that make the clearest difference to success, and channeled time, energy, and resources toward them.[9]

What are these pivotal jobs? Back when Ken was head of HR at Continental Airlines, CEO Gordon Bethune used to say, "If we don't have pilots, we're not in business." Talk about mission-critical talent! But the truth is that Continental's baggage handlers were in some ways equally crucial for creating customer value as the pilots. Yet in a different way. The point is that companies need a differentiated—and balanced— approach to talent management. One size does not fit all.

Which talent pools make the biggest difference in your organization? Much has been written on this topic, and there is no shortage of experts. But it's still really difficult to manage talent strategically. To get the process going, we often use a simple 2x2 matrix to map out the different talent pools of an organization. In the Figure 4.2 below, we've shown the grid for a [disguised] biotech firm and the spread of skill areas across two dimensions: strategic value and uniqueness.

In the upper right corner are "mission-critical" positions, central to the company's strategy and unique in some way (hard to find, hard to replace). These are "A" positions vital to the future success of the company. In the bottom right quadrant are different roles, central to strategic value, yes, but less unique and more generally available across other firms. They tend to be managed differently but are no less important to execution and value creation. In the top left quadrant are those with skills that are unique and complementary assets, but not necessarily central to the core strategy. In the bottom left are supporting roles whose work is more operational.

In our experience, each company has its own unique map, and the process of mapping gives executives insight into their talent configuration. Roles in each of these quadrants contribute in different ways to

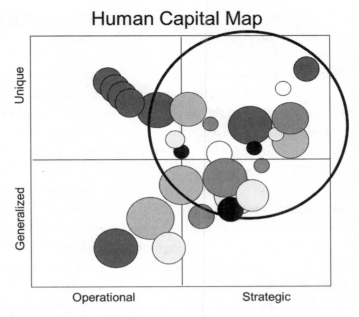

FIGURE 4.2 Human Capital Map

strategy execution. They need to be managed somewhat differently, and research backs this up.[10]

Executives who take a differentiated approach to talent management tend to have a more complete view of their organization, and this helps them avoid some of the symptoms of the talent syndrome. With a clearer view of key positions and roles, they can make more strategic investments as a result. Let's look at two such examples at Microsoft and SunTrust.

Microsoft: Create a differentiated talent model. In the tech sector—including Microsoft—some roles are very specialized. For example, some are internally facing, with responsibility for innovating and creating products and services, while others are externally facing, working with customers and partners. The diversity of roles, skills, and experiences requires a differentiated approach to talent. The highest priority tends to be placed on those whose skills are unique, specialized, hard to find, and hard to keep because they are in such high demand.

Microsoft's transformation depends on first identifying these talent pools, and then acquiring, developing, and managing them successfully.

At the same time, a differentiated approach to talent is needed because some work is focused on delivering today's business results, while others are critical for creating the future. Both today and tomorrow are important, but they are not the same. They have different time horizons when it comes to talent management and strategy execution. Microsoft's challenge is one of *ambidexterity*—how to deliver on today's business needs while simultaneously investing in tomorrow.[11]

"There is work we're doing today, whether it's legacy or current work that needs to continue to be done in an excellent way to advance. You need talented people doing that work," Joe Whittinghill, Microsoft's head of talent management, explained. "But you also have work that's way out on the far horizon where you may say, 'We need to get someone to come in and help us think about what's out there.' For example, the HoloLens [Microsoft's holographic computing platform], the people working on quantum computing, and so on." Key talent in that space "can really be a game changer" for the company, Whittinghill explained.

To initialize its talent management system, Microsoft develops a slate of mission-critical roles and talent pools that warrant special attention and priority. Each of the business leads does this for their own organization, and they are accountable for establishing plans to ensure appropriate talent against key business priorities. As the company looks to move into emerging spaces, say artificial intelligence or neuro-technology, they create a range of options for shoring up those skill pools.

Depending on the talent need, Microsoft deploys one of three solutions: buy, borrow or build. *Buying* means external hires "where we need fresh talent or strategic talent to serve a particular need," Whittinghill said. *Borrow* involves engaging vendors or partners to help get projects done or contract with gig staff to take on projects through a certain amount of time. And *build* "is your classic, we are going to need to develop people into the work force we need for the future."[12]

All three approaches have their merits, and Microsoft has learned the value of developing a differentiated model for its varied talent pools.

Their approach ensures they are in a much better position to have the right mix of skills available for today and tomorrow.

SunTrust: Be bullish on talent. In a related way, Bill Rogers faced a situation at SunTrust where he needed to make a big bet on pivotal, mission-critical talent. Recall, when he reconstituted his team, he placed Jerome Lienhard in charge of the mortgage business. This was a key decision because the mortgage division was an especially critical part of SunTrust's turnaround strategy. During the financial crisis, SunTrust was hit especially hard by the collapse in the mortgage sector, and that business had been hemorrhaging money. In 2010 alone, the mortgage business had lost more than $700 million.

Rogers had confidence in Lienhard because he had demonstrated exceptional personal and business leadership skills. But, ironically, Jerome had limited mortgage business experience, so he would need help.

The first order of business was to identify the most critical roles to ensure a successful turnaround of the business. These jobs ranged from capital markets to risk oversight and sales leadership. The lift needed was substantial, and without a team of "heroes" who had the ability to turn the mortgage business around, it would be an albatross, draining company resources and limiting the chances to go forward. In that event, SunTrust would need to seriously rethink its position in mortgages.

"Go big or go home—swing for the bleachers, Jerome." Channeling George Steinbrenner's classic decision to hire great sluggers into the New York Yankees ball club, Lienhard went out to find the best of the best in the industry. Do whatever it takes. This was admittedly a calculated risk. But in the end, Rogers and team decided that getting (merely) good people in those roles would not be enough—they needed great. The process required a deliberate and clear people strategy. Lienhard worked with his HR business partners to begin the search for the most knowledgeable and capable in the industry. They found some stellar talent, and drew them from Wall Street and the Federal Reserve.

This deliberate approach worked, producing a high return on investment. Within two years, the new mortgage all-star team fixed the underperforming problems and built a foundation for growth, transforming substantial losses into net positive earnings in the following years.

The Microsoft and SunTrust examples showcase the importance of a differentiated approach to talent management. Each of our profile companies makes similar distinctions among their portfolio of human capital, recognizing that some positions are mission critical (although they would also hasten to add that nobody is unimportant). For example, UPS recognizes its district and regional managers are the backbone of the company, but so are their drivers—nobody has more impact on customers' satisfaction and brand differentiation. Marriott sees general managers of its hotels as pivotal positions, not because they are high ranking, but because they are the center of the hub of the business.

Have you identified these mission-critical roles in your organization? Is the norm for talent management to manage everyone the same? Our stories show there are many different ways to tackle this challenge. Some organizations start by analyzing the role and contribution of each position in their firm. A 2×2 human capital map or other documentation makes mission-critical roles visible, the first step in developing a strategic talent management process.

Other companies start by evaluating the strengths and weaknesses in their business. Where are their biggest growth opportunities? Where is the market moving? What must they do to leapfrog the competition? Clearly defining your organization's business needs and prospects, then determining the critical talent required, is another effective approach. No matter the path you take, the point is to delineate your talent management strategy. It takes time, critical thinking, and a willingness to take risks. But the return on your investment in talent differentiation will be consistently higher as a result.

How Are You Assessing Your Bench?

Once you have identified mission-critical roles for strategy execution, do you have the bench of talent to take on those responsibilities? This kind of talent review may seem like a pretty obvious one-two combination, but recall that the "talent syndrome" is characterized by a chronic shortage of talent to meet business needs. And to sustain executional excellence, organizations must assess not only the team in place but also the bench for the future.

Microsoft: Connect talent and business reviews. Microsoft has made these kinds of talent reviews a high priority. They combine business assessment and people assessment. "We ask ourselves, do we have key talent in the most critical jobs and do we have the right talent?" CHRO Kathleen Hogan explained. "We spend a lot of time on that. In fact, Satya has often said, 'It all comes down to talent.'"

To make certain that Microsoft has a deep bench of up-and-coming leaders to manage key projects and business opportunities, Nadella and team conduct a series of talent reviews, or "Talent Talks" as they call them. These reviews start within each of the businesses—at a local level from engineering to sales to corporate functions—to review employees, discuss opportunities to redeploy people up and across teams, and develop growth experiences. As they roll up, the Talent Talks serve as preparation for a final set of reviews with Nadella, his direct reports, and their senior HR leader.

Talent Talks have been instrumental for several reasons. They give Microsoft a window to its leadership capability and bench strength. Does the available talent match the overall business needs? The sessions also shine a light on diversity and inclusion and feed ongoing succession plans.

But the reviews go beyond talent alone and underscore strategy execution. It is a great time for the leader and the CEO to have a conversation about how their business strategy is translating into their organization strategy. Rather than just an HR review, a people review, Whittinghill said, "we feel that adding in the organizational and strategy component—along with the talent review—allows Satya to get a much more complete picture of what is happening in that organization."

The tie-in to strategy and business reviews helps to sharpen priorities. "We've become more sophisticated in the talent management world about focusing on what's important versus everything," Whittinghill said. After each review, managers agree on a set of key time-dependent actions that will be taken to drive talent management forward. (And, because it's Microsoft, there's an online tracking system to support the action/updates.) "That discipline of execution around documenting, agreeing on, and follow-up on actions is just as important as everything else that we do," he explained. The approach has the effect of keeping the conversations continuous and evergreen. "We don't see this as an event. We see this as a review that happens during our year-long cycle of executing talent management all the time."

Nadella spends more than a week on Talent Talks each year, along with his fourteen direct reports. "That's how important human capital management is to us," Whittinghill said, noting Nadella's belief that "we need to manage for today, but we need to keep our eye on the future as well."

The takeaway: Integrating talent reviews with business reviews takes time and discipline, but the payoff is a leadership bench that's connected into real-time and future business needs.

SunTrust: Focus on your top talent. To get to the next level of performance, SunTrust made some difficult talent decisions. As CEO Rogers noted:

> It used to be that maybe if you were skilled at your craft and you were an okay leader that might be enough to get by. But that's just not acceptable anymore, and the transparency shows it. We have augmented our ability to identify and grow top talent. We conduct teammate engagement surveys. We complete talent reviews and succession planning. As a result, there's so much more information. You can clearly see it—you can see "good" and you can see "average." We've coined a phrase that "we're going from better to best," but the gold standard has to be "best."

In 2012, Rogers and team implemented a new talent review system, assessing managers on both current performance and their potential to succeed at the next levels of leadership. The goal was to identify the next cadre of future leaders, and also guide development of those suited for their current role but not [yet] for the role three years out.

SunTrust's talent review sessions focused on their priority attributes of a leader. As noted earlier, Rogers recognized the importance of modeling these behaviors with his team, and having candid discussions on an ongoing basis with each of his direct reports. Rogers and the executive team instituted quarterly half-day talent planning sessions dedicated to

All in all, Marriott's talent development process is a reflection of how they run their business, supporting their associate-first culture.

SunTrust: Develop insights. In this chapter, we've discussed a number of effective talent management processes. Done well, they benefit the companies and top talent that work there. One of the win-wins is high-performer engagement and retention. Another is that the talent will be ready when their time is needed. Let's look at one more example aimed at this kind of specific opportunity.

Several years ago, Rogers and SunTrust launched an innovative process for high-potential Gen X and Millennial midlevel leaders. "Insights" was established as a fifteen-month program to complement SunTrust's regular talent programs, with a few unique features. First, it helped to shine a light on a team of thirty to thirty-five diverse, high-potential young leaders across all disciplines and functions of the bank. While most programs focus on individuals, Insights was designed to take a cohort approach to development.

The process began with a set of criteria used by senior executives to nominate and select individuals for the program. Once in the Insights cohort, the members met with senior executives in small rotating groups. The open discussions centered on different leadership responsibilities and perspectives to help Insights members prepare and understand the terrain of a senior leader. They got candid feedback (and provided candid feedback to the senior leaders in return). The program blended personal, team, thought, and business leadership development through virtual, classroom, and mostly experiential learning. And it provided exposure to all businesses, functions, executives, and board members.

Since 2012, more than ninety high-potential leaders have successfully completed the program. And in a highly competitive industry where talented people have ample opportunity, more than 95 percent of them stayed at SunTrust. "Just imagine seven to ten years from now when there are over three hundred of these diverse, highly developed, talented teams of leaders driving the business forward," Rogers said. "Given their deep understanding of SunTrust and the industry joined together with the strong networks they've developed over the years, the return on our investment should be significant and long lasting."

There is a lot to learn from this program. When you engage high potentials directly with the CEO and senior leadership team—and with each other—you strengthen the individuals and your company. You are building the base of talent, strengthening the culture, and building a more solid foundation for future capability.

Let's take a step back. We've tackled a lot in this section. The examples from Vail, Marriott, Microsoft, and SunTrust demonstrate there are many different ways to produce and perpetuate your pipeline of talent. While the solutions must be tailored to your organizations, the principles are the same: pinpoint mission-critical positions, design a robust talent review process, manage and create development programs that reinforce your business needs and culture. And integrate these elements so they work as a system.

We'll shift now to the third major "Ability" lever for execution: collaborative capability.

COLLABORATION IS A TALENT MULTIPLIER

Collaboration may be one of the most frequently used words in organizations today. And for good reason. In our increasingly connected world, individual talent alone will not suffice. The time spent by managers and employees in collaborative activities has ballooned by more than 50 percent over the past two decades.[14]

In the context of strategy execution, collaboration is a requirement for joint decision making, pooling resources, and sequencing actions to drive performance. And it's the inability to collaborate effectively that most often derails execution—a point we made in the previous chapter on Alignment.

But collaborative capability is also a "talent multiplier." What does that mean? Academics often refer to it as *human capital leverage*. Professional service firms have long understood the power of collaboration as the basis of their business model. Senior professionals with vast experience partner with junior associates to spread their knowledge over more projects, clients, and opportunities. Their clients win because they get better counsel at a lower cost. The firm wins because they get the most out of their team. And the employees win because they maximize their contribution while growing and learning from others across the firm.

Are You Connecting Your Power Source?

But collaboration as a talent multiplier is more than teamwork. It goes beyond the willingness of individuals to cooperate. It depends crucially on developing shared understanding and collective knowledge. Think about the highest performing teams you've seen. Flight crews, firefighters, ER units, and the like work together in a synchronized manner seemingly with one mind, what scholars call *transactive memory*, based on their deep understanding of the others' expertise, both domain knowledge and architectural knowledge (how they fit together).[15]

That's the starting point for collaborative capability. More generally, collaborative relationships like this can be conduits of mutual knowledge sharing and learning. The capacity to leverage these networks increases the knowledge base of individuals around the organization— effectively multiplying their talent. Some evidence suggests that the associated social capital may be as important as human capital for driving performance. You can again see the potential connections between Ability and Alignment in this aspect of strategic execution.

As we go through the examples below, check yourself against these questions:

- How well do managers and employees work together to make everyone better?
- Do teams have discretion to make decisions and act using their best judgement?
- Is there a spirit of collaboration that cuts across business units and functions?

Marriott: Together We're Better. When Marriott's acquisition of Starwood was announced, Sorenson championed the vision of "Together We're Better." But achieving that ideal of corporate unity, postacquisition, is never easy. Most experts agree that when integration fails, it fails because of people issues, typically around culture.[16]

"I think when M&A deals fail culturally, it's because companies don't take the time to listen to both sides and figure out what makes sense," said CHRO David Rodriguez. He saw this an opportunity for Marriott and Starwood to learn from one another to create a better overall company. "Sometimes it's not going to be how Marriott does things that's going to be the best way. It's going to be something that Starwood is doing." For example, Starwood's loyalty program was top-rated in the hotel industry. The Marriott team embraced Starwood's design-forward approach and personalized mobile app experience, taking the best of their program to up Marriott's game overall.[17]

A little less talk, and a lot more action. To kick-start execution and build momentum quickly, the integration team decided not to distract the organization with abstract conceptual discussions about cultural differences. Instead they focused on how best practices and innovations from both companies could be deployed across the new enterprise. Senior leaders hosted a series of three-day general manager conferences in collaboration with each of the continent presidents. The conferences were the first opportunity for Marriott and Starwood managers to come together and take a hands-on approach to begin building a mutual network. They emphasized "Together We're Better," discussing integration progress, challenges, business issues, and brand strategies. They encouraged information exchange and ways of working together.

They also created Gateway, an onboarding system for all employees. More than just a class, notebook, or briefing, Gateway was launched as a year-long experience that takes employees through aspects of culture, teamwork, learning the craft, and building a future together. Not only does the system facilitate accelerated engagement, it also provides concrete activities and resources to strengthen personal connections across the organization. The goal was to bridge the cultures, enable better team cohesion, and energize performance.

To further build collaboration, the integration team conducted informal learning sessions in advance of formal training with all Starwood and Marriott employees in locations such as New York, London, or Shanghai. The goal was to allow team members in different geographies to form personal bonds and begin working together early. Instead of asking the employees from the two companies to just "get along," the sessions provided a common experience of working together—learning from each other—from which they could build. Following these inter-actions, Marriott rolled out operating systems training in areas such as guest registration, revenue management, and the like.

Ultimately, these initiatives helped create enterprise-wide engage-ment around the newly integrated Marriott family of brands. This has been an important challenge. In interviews with general managers about their work, virtually all Marriott GMs—regardless of brand—mentioned Marriott International or the Marriott family. Whether they came from Ritz Carlton, JW Marriott, or Renaissance—all brands within Marriott International—the GMs felt a strong connection to the overall moth-ership. That wasn't the case with Starwood managers, whose affinities were more with the former Starwood brands such as Westin, Sheraton, and St. Regis. For those leaders, building a connected perspective with the Marriott enterprise—or any enterprise—was not second nature. But Sorenson and team felt that such a connection was critical to their "To-gether We're Better" vision.

Technology has also played a role. In addition to creating face-to-face opportunities for leaders and employees to build collaborative capability as a team, Marriott created an online integration hub, infor-mation repository, and collaboration portal to support the newly com-bined work force. The Marriott Platform was based on feedback from employee pulse surveys, which showed separation in pockets of the or-ganization: places where networks were not developing. The Platform includes updates on the Marriott-Starwood integration, basic company information, success stories, messages from senior leaders, and other helpful material for employees. Accessible via mobile devices, the Plat-form is a timely tool that has improved communication consistency. GMs have found it particularly useful for keeping in touch with em-ployees in their hotels.

Marriott executives recognized that it takes time to get everyone working together and truly maximize the potential ability of the two combined organizations. What can we learn from their journey? First, the intangible elements of culture integration and collaborative capa-bility come about by managing the very tangible aspects of work. In that regard, it is important to be concrete and direct, not abstract and theoretical. Second, create multiple forums for overt collaboration—in person, across the global leadership team, at the local level. Third, where possible, leverage technology as a go-to resource to allow shared learnings and timely, consistent communication. Marriott has been very purposeful with a long-term view of capability development. Their investment in better strategic execution is paying off.

UPS: Collaboration is our business. Like Marriott, collaboration is an integral part of the UPS business model. The company has always been an integrator of buyers and sellers, shippers and receivers, creating shared value through supply chain logistics. As the company has grown globally, particularly in emerging markets, the importance of collaboration with external partners has become both important and more challenging.

Because UPS is a network of shipping outlets and services, every node in the network is connected to all the others. That added complexity makes collaboration more difficult. Any change in one node has a potential ripple affect multiplied exponentially across the entire network, with a profound impact on the ability to execute. Those nodes consist of people who need to know the UPS system and how to make it work in different environments.

In emerging markets particularly, UPS has to find the right external partners to help them apply their processes, procedures, and rigorous customer standards in the context of local and regional country, government, and business challenges, norms, and requirements. Consistency is key. "When we go into a country and have a partnership relationship, we're running a network business where one of the paramount value adds of our business is that it should look and feel the same way across the entire network no matter where it is," said Jim Barber, president of UPS International. It's not an easy task, and it has to be right from the get-go to execute their strategy. "Usually when something goes wrong, it has to do with the initial steps of the relationships being out of kilter," Barber said. Governance, contractual constraints, and legal systems issues can hamstring the situation, making relationships difficult. Security and compliance are also problematic at times.

So how does UPS forge its partnerships? It starts with being gracious and respectful—especially in the local environment. Barber said the UPS team respects the fact that they are a guest in each country, and maintains that respect. They listen, they learn, and they look for opportunities to collaborate. But they also are clear where no compromises will be made. "In many emerging markets, what is normal in those markets can be abnormal all the way up to illegal in the markets that we come from," Barber explained.

Finding areas of common ground and getting partners to focus on delivering high UPS standards is key. Their operating model helps make that happen. The Emerging Markets team includes the local management team who runs the business on a day-to-day basis, plus a SWOT (strengths, weaknesses, opportunities, threats) team they can call on when needed. If there is a situation the local team can't handle, the SWOT team goes in, collaborating with the local partner to determine the root cause and fix the problem. The bias is to help the local team so they can continue as a high-performing node. But if that can't happen, the SWOT team may recommend removal of the node, or replacement of the local team.

A lot rides on having the right leadership team—at the local level and as UPS partners. They must work together to create a successful node that can deliver UPS standards and serve customers in very diverse environments. That responsibility typically falls to a district manager and a country manager. Barber said that "they are *the* jobs," noting these leaders collaborate to teach the UPS way and determine how to apply it in that market. He further explained they "put very skilled UPSers who have a background and know what 'greatness' looks like to convert that new team [and bring them] on board into the fold." Leveraging the local partnership, they work closely to create the collaborative system required for success. When that happens, Barber said "we leave a team of UPSers in there that will have a place forever."

Creating teams of local talent that partner with strong UPS leaders has allowed UPS to grow successfully around the world. Their system of collaboration has multiplied talent in every market, generating great returns for the company. In their view, there is perhaps no more important lesson for strategy execution.

This example from UPS and the one from Marriott both reveal a couple of important takeaways. First, it's not just that collaboration is important. Virtually no one would disagree with that in principle. It's that collaborative capability is best developed and reinforced *in situ*, in practice, in the context of where the work is happening.

Second, it's not merely a matter of establishing good will or positive intent. Just as with prioritizing investments in mission-critical positions, it's important to identify where the critical connections are needed in your business and focus collaboration there. In the Marriott example, it was the point of integration for the Starwood acquisition. In the UPS example, it was with external partners. Although their approaches are different, the lesson learned is the same.

WHERE DO YOU STAND?

Just like in the previous chapter on Alignment, we hope you do two things at the end of this chapter. First, assess yourself on the key elements of Ability. But second, remember that the Ability factors are only one part of the ecosystem of the 4A framework.

Take a few minutes to do a realistic self-assessment, using the checklist below (Table 4.1). Compare yourself to the examples we shared. In some cases, you may be ahead of the game. In places where you're behind, or God forbid not even in the game, use the lessons learned by these companies to begin a dialogue with others in your organization about the causes and consequences of Ability gaps. Then start to identify the best path forward to improvement.

Leadership

What is the state of leadership in your organization? In this chapter, we didn't simply extol the virtues of leadership. Platitudes, even good ones, won't move the needle on executional excellence. From the top down, leadership needs to embody the key elements of strategy; the technical and functional requirements, the business imperatives, as well as the cultural and personal qualities of the organization. These leaders are the outward and visible signs of the company's internal execution capability.

TABLE 4.1 Ability Checklist

ABILITY CHECKLIST	
Leadership	1. Our leaders have the skills, competencies, and experience needed for breakthrough performance.
	2. We develop a continual flow of "next generation" leaders who are capable of leading us to the future.
	3. Our leaders inspire and empower others to achieve organizational goals.
Talent	4. We have a robust talent management system to identify, develop, and retain high-quality employees.
	5. High-priority, "mission-critical" positions are filled by our top performers.
	6. Managers spend time coaching and developing their employees and teams.
Collaboration	7. Managers and employees work well together to make everyone better.
	8. Teams have discretion to make decisions and act using their best judgement.
	9. There is a spirit of collaboration that cuts across business units and functions.

© Scott A. Snell and Kenneth J. Carrig

How well does the team operate? In complex companies, the team often supplants the individual because no one person can carry the organization. Execution is a collective sport, and the ability of team members to support one another and bring out the best is a prerequisite for aligned performance. The best companies are constantly assessing their leadership talent to ensure the right combinations.

Talent Pipeline

There is a wonderful quote attributed to Abraham Lincoln: "Give me six hours to chop down a tree and I will spend the first four sharpening the axe." His point is that execution depends on preparation. To execute well today, you have to have prepared yesterday.

How robust is your talent pipeline? We are continually amazed when companies fall victim to the talent syndrome because they haven't done the very reasonable work necessary to build a talent pipeline. They need to make sure their best people are in the most critical jobs. And they need to focus on the future, the needs of the business going forward. Your talent pipeline will shape what's possible and what's not.

Remember, there are a variety of ways to help people develop, some formal and some informal. We have found that helping people develop is a real-time, never-ending duty of leaders as coaches. Does your organization have an integrated learning and development strategy?

Collaborative Capability

The twin sister of Alignment is collaboration. One is required for the other. And companies continue to struggle. There are powerful forces pulling away Alignment and defeating collaboration. Good intentions are not sufficient. Have you hardwired collaborative capability at the most critical junctions required for your strategy? Often it is cross-functional collaboration that stymies organizations. Other times it's partners in a value stream. The point is to identify which connections are most important and make it easy for the collaboration to take place.

WHAT NEXT? BUILDING ORGANIZATIONAL CAPABILITY: ARCHITECTURE

Remember, the 4A model is a system of interrelated and interdependent factors. By design, we've echoed several points about Alignment in this chapter on Ability. But as you know, executional capability is more than just about Alignment and Ability. It also requires infrastructure, processes, structure, and systems to make things scalable and repeatable. In the next chapter, we cover the Architecture element of the 4A framework, delving into aspects of organizational design.

5 ARCHITECTURE

The Clarity of Design and Process

WE'VE DISCUSSED the strategic opportunities of Marriott's integration with Starwood and the challenges of marrying up the two organizations. We've highlighted the importance of combined leadership, talent, cultures, and collaborative capability. But equally important, and perhaps more vexing in the short term, is the task of harmonizing its different operating systems, technologies, structures, and processes. Arne Sorenson sees the Starwood acquisition as an opportunity to transform Marriott, and has repeatedly noted that if the merger only creates a bigger hotel chain, that will be a disappointment to everyone. His goal is a *better* Marriott, a company that operates differently, creating more value for customers by developing better capabilities, more choices, more touch points, and a richer connection that can evolve with loyal customers. What's the right organizational design to achieve those objectives?

SunTrust, too, worked through its own integration of businesses acquired over the years into a unified portfolio. Bill Rogers had the challenge of blending separate geographic regions, lines of business, and functions into a unified whole. One important lesson learned along the way was that as circumstances change, the organization architecture may need to change, too. What worked well in the past may not work for the future, and SunTrust's architecture prior to the financial crisis would not be adequate as the bank came out of it. Rogers's goal was to streamline SunTrust's organization, strip away inefficiencies, reduce costs, and create a more finely tuned operation. And going forward, what would be the best way to organize SunTrust to simultaneously create more efficiency and more value for clients?

UPS has faced somewhat different architectural challenges. As the company grew internationally and faced the complexities of global markets, it needed a broader network that included comprehensive logistics and supply chain capabilities as well as traditional package delivery. At the same time, UPS's economic model has shifted as e-commerce altered the balance from traditional business-to-business (B2B) transactions to business-to-consumers (B2C). In the past, when the bulk of UPS deliveries were large-volume B2B, the margins and network requirements for that business model were more manageable. As more consumers began ordering from Amazon and other online retailers, the network requirements expanded, and the margins on smaller deliveries were smaller. Alan Gershenhorn, the company's chief commercial officer, described it this way: "The economics of shipping to homes is not as good as shipping to businesses. But there's unlimited opportunity. It's a challenge because we know it's the future." UPS had always been an organization focused on efficiency, and now the requirements were increasing.

The management teams at Marriott, SunTrust, and UPS—indeed all of the organizations in our research—recognize that organization architecture has a profound impact on execution. The design of infrastructure, processes, systems, and controls directly shapes behavior and performance. In the best of cases, that impact is extremely positive, and the organization architecture aids efficiency, clarity, and ease of operations. The appropriate design can effectively propel performance by channeling resources, informing better decisions, and supporting collective action.

And, unfortunately, the impact of architecture can be negative, where bureaucracy, inefficient processes, and cumbersome systems impede performance. In Chapter 2 we cautioned that the impact of organization architecture can be positive or negative, but it is rarely neutral. We would reinforce that point again here.

In this chapter, we'll cover some of the key priorities in managing an organization's architecture, what can go wrong, and what needs to go right. We'll diagnose some of the causes and effects of poor architecture, reasons why people end up working in silos, disconnected from others, impairing decisions and dragging performance. We also address ways to clean up the organization architecture, creating better efficiency of operations, streamlining processes, and using intelligent systems to support better decision making and behavior.

As legendary architect Frank Lloyd Wright once observed, "We create our buildings and then they create us." The same is true of organization architecture. The design of your organization is one of the key determinants of organizational behavior, how people engage one another, and what they are able to accomplish together. In that regard, architecture influences what organizations are capable of achieving, what's actually possible with regard to strategy execution.

Throughout this book, we've emphasized that the challenges of execution are multifaceted and interconnected. Perhaps nowhere is that more obvious than in how the organization architecture affects performance. Because the design of the organization influences authority structures and information flows, its impact on decision making, behavior, and performance is substantial. The form and configuration of that Architecture either supports or impedes Alignment, Ability, and Agility.

SYMPTOMS OF POOR FORM AND FUNCTION

We've often heard the axiom "Form follows function," meaning that the shape or design of your architecture will—or should—be based on its intended purpose or function. In theory, an architectural design incorporates everything it needs to support its purpose with no waste or extraneous elements to detract from it. Form follows function. In reality, the opposite is also true—"Function follows form." The organization operates the way it is designed. And, as they say, every organization is perfectly designed to get the results it is now getting. If we want different results, we may need a different architecture. Unfortunately, many of the performance problems we see in organizations stem from its architecture.[1]

What are some of the symptoms of a dysfunctional architecture? And what can you do about it? Let's start with three biggies.

Symptom #1: Are You Repeatedly Letting Your Customer Down?

Does your organization consistently come up short in its promises to customers? We're not talking about customers who want something you don't offer. If you run a diner and customers ask for chateaubriand, that's a strategic choice, not an execution failing. We're talking about situations where you've ostensibly offered something to customers but don't deliver—or can't deliver. When this happens repeatedly, there may be an architectural problem.

Imagine an airline that frequently loses luggage, oversells flights, or has chronic delays and mechanical and safety problems. Or a medical center with poor clinical procedures, medical malpractice, lost patient data, or repeated administrative and billing errors. We can probably all tell our sordid experiences where organizations destroy value this way, and as customers of those organizations we may have gotten miffed at the people involved. But the reality is that these performance problems were probably not just the result of disaffected employees, although there may be a contributing factor. More than likely there was something systemically wrong in the organization architecture.

W. Edwards Deming famously estimated that 94 percent of performance problems are systems problems, not people problems. And, "A bad system will beat a good person, every time." The reality is that motivated and talented people can compensate for bad organization architecture in the short run, but not for long. Why? Because the architecture ultimately determines *how the work gets done*. The structures, processes, systems, and controls are the tools we use to drive organizational performance. Nothing much good comes out of a bad system. If we want different results, we need to fix the underlying system.[2]

Symptom #2: Are You Working in Silos?

One of the frustrations we hear most from managers and employees is that their organizations are siloed and executives operate in their own fiefdoms. These little islands of power can grow into pretty big landmasses, bloated with headcount, duplicated functions, duplicated resources, and added cost. And as leaders try to optimize their own operations, the overall enterprise can suffer.

We touched on this in the chapter on Alignment, but the crux of the problem here is that the alignment problems are typically rooted in and reinforced by poor organizational architecture. Here's how: every structure creates demarcations and separations; lines in the organization that can become cracks, fissures, or fault lines, especially when they are reinforced by internal processes, systems, and budgetary controls. Organizational design choices are often driven by very rational considerations of scale and efficiency, which is all well and good. We're all for efficiency—specialized division of labor is one of the most important principles of formal organization.[3]

Execution problems occur when decisions and workflow need to transcend across those organizational boundaries, but don't. The reality is that most of the critical execution problems require cross-functional solutions. Product development, for example, requires input from R&D, operations, finance, marketing, and so on. Customer service requires the interface of sales, accounting, supply, and distribution. When the organizational design makes collective decision making and coordination difficult, the organization gets stymied. You've likely seen it yourself.

There are two related problems here. First, when coordination breaks down, duplication builds up. Have you ever noticed that organizational inefficiencies tend to grow at the spaces between organizational units? Administrative tasks get duplicated, resources are hoarded, information flows break down, communication falters, and interests diverge. Creeping bureaucracy is an artifact of using policy to deal with these uncertainties of inefficient operations. Second, when coordination breaks down, isolation leads to territorial declarations of "That's not my job," "That's not your call," and so forth. If roles and responsibilities are unclear, then decision authority and accountabilities become uncertain. The result is organizational slippage. Have you ever experienced a situation where a critical issue in your organization was left unattended because nobody owned it or took responsibility? Opportunities can slip by you, or problems go unresolved.

Throughout this book, we've continued to come back to the importance of collaboration for execution: not just the willingness to work together, but the ability to jointly identify and solve problems. But alignment and good intentions are not enough. Even when individuals resolve to work collaboratively, the wrong organization architecture can make their efforts seem like an unnatural act. Managers routinely tell us that despite their best efforts, execution gets entangled or bogged down in the organization's outdated bureaucracy. Reporting requirements, decision rights, processes, resource allocation, workflows, and information systems appropriate for a different purpose or a different time can seem like a morass of rules, policies, and administrative sludge that obviate performance. And when processes and systems are antiquated or confounding, the problems multiply. What's your experience?

Symptom #3: Are You Flying Blind?

The third symptom of a dysfunctional architecture has to do with information availability. Here's a quick analogy: When a pilot flies in good weather, s/he can operate under what's called VFR (visual flight rules), meaning the pilot can see where the plane is going relative to the ground and other planes. In that instance, the pilot has all the information needed to simply execute the flight plan as submitted before take-off. However, when the weather is poor, the pilot needs to switch to IFR (instrument flight rules), where onboard avionics provide real-time information about weather systems, air traffic, and other hazards to compensation for poor visibility. Under IFR, the pilot needs constant information and support to make adjustments in the flight plan. Without it, the pilot—and others—are in danger.

Is the parallel to organizations obvious? We often hear from managers and employees that one of their biggest execution challenges is that they don't have adequate information they need to carry out the plan or adjust the plan as needed. "We're flying blind," they say. They're committed to the mission and have all the skills and experience necessary, but often don't have the latest information needed to act.

Has this ever happened to you? There are three chief reasons for this lapse. First, as situations change, hierarchical structures and authority systems often require that individuals go up the chain of command for approval. That can take time and can be slowed when higher-ups don't have the information they need as well. Or when decision rights are not clear, the process can bog down. Second, broken or inefficient processes leave gaps in information flows and communication, resulting in one person having critical resources another needs, but no obvious way to connect the dots. Third, information systems, despite their name, often don't provide the information or data support people need to make decisions. There is broad frustration among those on the front line that these systems are designed for reporting, not informing. In other words, the flow of information goes to the bosses, but not to those on the front line who are responsible for executing the strategy.

There's one other cause for concern, and it has as much to do with alignment as it does architecture. When senior leaders make operational changes, budget adjustments, personnel changes, and the like, it may not necessarily change the strategy, but it can affect the way the strategy needs to be carried out. When this happens, and others are not fully informed, things break down. Who hasn't experienced a situation where individuals plead, "I wasn't in the loop!" Research by Booz and Company found that information flows and decision rights were the two most fundamental causes of breakdown in strategy execution. And that breakdown can be traced back to the organization architecture. The consensus from executives in our research supports this conclusion as well.[4]

WHAT CAN YOU DO?

Each of these symptoms emanates from the fact that organizational architectures are complex systems, and any approach to strategy execution has to take that complexity into account. Dealing with organizational complexity is challenging because, while it may make things difficult, we don't want to eliminate complexity per se. Some complexity is the result of inefficiencies and waste. Let's agree to find the best ways to remove those excesses. But some complexity is inevitable—even necessary—for organizations to operate in complex environments. Systems theorists refer to this as the "law of requisite variety." Every system needs to reflect the complexity of the environment in which it operates. Otherwise, it cannot respond to the diversity of problems and opportunities it faces. At the same time, we want to reduce the confusion and uncertainty that arises from complexity.[5]

So as we go through the chapter, our goal is not so much to convince you to eliminate organization complexity—it's not that simple. Rather, the organization architecture helps you *manage* that complexity in your organization by putting guardrails on things so they don't get out of hand. Our experience, research, executive roundtables, and company case studies all suggests that there are three key levers, and the right interventions can set the organization in a positive direction:

- Clarify your operating model.
- Streamline your organizational design.
- Create an intelligent architecture that enables better decision making.

Each of these points requires further elaboration, and not only do they combine together, they are intertwined with the other elements of the 4A model. Let's dig into each.

CLARIFY YOUR OPERATING MODEL

In our Alignment chapter, we emphasized the criticality of clarifying the strategic intent of your organization; its purpose, core identity, and direction. Doing so helps the executive team achieve horizontal alignment and sets the stage to strengthen vertical alignment by translating strategy into operational priorities. Even as companies take these steps, it's surprising how many still struggle to clarify their operating model—that is, identifying the set of core capabilities that drive value, and the underlying processes, systems, skills, and structures that support it.

As we noted in Chapter 2, we think of the operating model as an *architectural blueprint* for strategy execution. Take for example when Tom Monaghan created Domino's Pizza. He didn't just have a different strategy for pizza delivery (thirty minutes or it's free); he had a different operating model. Instead of using chefs to lovingly knead the dough by hand and carefully apply the toppings, he borrowed assembly line processes to construct pizzas in advance. And instead of using tradi-tional wood-fired brick ovens to bake the pizza, he used conveyer tech-nology that kept the temperature uniform and reduced baking time to around six minutes. Instead of building restaurants for in-store dining, he stamped out smaller shops and incentivized drivers to deliver pizzas to customers at home. Did Monaghan make a better pizza? No way—that wasn't the goal. Did he change the pizza industry? Most certainly.

In many organizations, perhaps including yours, the operating model is more elaborate than Domino's original design. And most of the companies with which we have worked have multifaceted business models. It can get confusing trying to sort out the combination of ca-pabilities, processes, systems, structures, and skills that all contribute to value creation. We understand. And that's why it's so important to clar-ify your operating model to focus execution. In a recent study by Bain & Company only 20 percent of executives felt their operating models pro-vided them a competitive advantage. It stands to reason that most con-sider evolving their operating model as a top priority. The payoff can be substantial—the Bain study found that companies with a clear, robust operating model had better revenue growth and operating margins than those that did not.[6]

Why? There are three reasons. First, clarifying your operating model helps delineate the boundaries of the organization and strategy. You can't execute to achieve breakthrough performance without it. As we'll illustrate below with Marriott and UPS, these companies consciously evaluate the scope and composition of the business to determine which activities are most critical for value creation (and which are not). Sec-ond, your operating model sets conditions for the design of organi-zational architecture. It shines a light on the characteristics of your current organization that are critical for strategy execution, and there-fore should be reinforced or enhanced with the appropriate infrastruc-ture. It also reveals those elements of the architecture that might impede strategy execution and need to be fixed or eliminated. Third, a clear operating model helps prioritize execution. Instead of using a "peanut butter" approach to allocate resources, spreading too little investment over too many priorities, a focused operating model helps to crystalize which initiatives will have the biggest impact on performance. Strategy is about making choices, and a clear operating model helps to prioritize which decisions and which investments matter most.

As we go through this section, ask yourself the following questions:

- Is our operating model clear so that we know which core capabilities drive the most value to customers?
- For each capability, have we identified the underlying processes, systems, skills, and structures that are critical to drive performance?
- Have we prioritized key areas for investment to enhance our capability system for the future?

These questions all center on clarifying your operating model as a first step in designing the organization architecture. And they tie directly back to our prior discussions about organization alignment. That's the reality of execution—each aspect of the 4A framework is interconnected and mutually supportive.

Which Capabilities Matter Most—and Which Don't?

Here's an exercise you might try with your management team. Ask them: "Five years into the future, what will our customers require of us; that is, how will our value proposition change?" (You might be surprised by how hard it is to get agreement on this.) Then ask, "What set of four to six core capabilities will be required to deliver on this value proposition, and to what extent are they new?" Finally ask, "What processes, systems, skills, and structures are critical for building an architecture to support these capabilities?"

A simple set of questions, and a surprisingly difficult task to find the answers. What makes the task so difficult? Each of the questions represents a different part of your operating model. What's difficult is not deciding what to include; it's what to exclude or at least deemphasize. Every capability, process, structure, system, and so on is a candidate for inclusion, because at some level each may matter to the business. But, as they say, if everything is a priority, then nothing is a priority. The truth is that not every capability is equally critical to value creation. And not every process, system, or structural element is equally important for

moving the needle on performance. As we said in Chapter 2, to focus resources on execution, it is important to clarify which ones matter most
and which ones do not.

How do you do this? Begin with the customer value proposition.
You may find it useful to initially focus on three generic dimensions:
product leadership, operational excellence, and customer intimacy. Inevitably, most organizations land on some combination of these three. It
is very difficult to deliver all three at a world-class level, but it is difficult
to survive if you're not proficient at each.[7]

Next, identify the capabilities that make up your value chain, or
value network. Separate out those capabilities that are "table stakes"
in your industry: necessary but not sufficient to excel. Work to win-
now down the list to a small number that are most crucial. Most experts agree that organizations benefit by focusing on a small number
of capabilities. The Federal Emergency Management Agency (FEMA)
lists thirty-two on its website.[8] We find that number to be excessive, not
because it wouldn't be good to excel at all those things, but because the
sheer scope makes it difficult to focus execution priorities. Has FEMA
had difficulties executing in the past?

Which metrics are most useful for assessing how well you are performing each capability, and the degree to which you have created
customer value? Do these metrics comprise your strategy dashboard?
Again, don't proliferate your scorecard with myriad metrics. Like every
other aspect of this exercise, the challenge is to rein in complexity by
prioritizing only those that are most critical.

Marriott: Evolve the customer value proposition. In Figure 5.1,
we show a simplified depiction of Marriott's operating model. Over the
years, Marriott has adapted its operating model to emphasize what it
has seen as the most critical drivers of customer value. It divested its
business interests in restaurants, airline catering, amusement parks,
cruise lines, vacation clubs, and the like to focus on hotel management,
franchising, and customer relationships. Marriott even spun off its real
estate business (splitting with Host-Marriott in 1993) and actually owns
very few of its hotel properties.

Marriott Operating Model

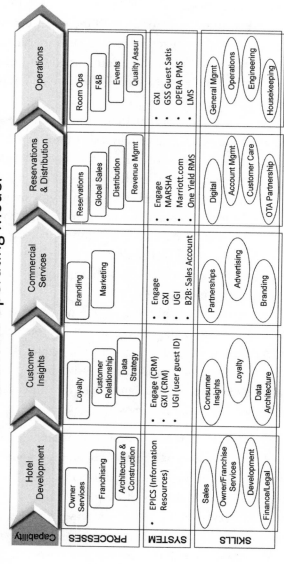

FIGURE 5.1 Marriott Operating Model
Source: Marriott International. Reprinted with permission.

Why? Because the key to Marriott's success is not the physical assets, but the intangible assets of service and customer care. As Ty Breland put it, "Our business is managing and relationships. It's not real estate." Marriott works with hotel property owners in two principal ways: either it has management contracts to develop and run the hotels or it franchises to hotel developers who then license Marriott brands, processes, and systems. In the cases where Marriott manages the properties, it employs all the personnel. In cases where it franchises to others, the franchisees must adhere to very strict standards of conduct and performance. Either way, Marriott builds its architecture around the key elements of execution and maintains almost total control over the look and feel of hotel operations and customer experience. It does this without incurring the risks of hotel ownership. And the fact that the company has a steady stream of franchise fees and management contracts helps it smooth out exposure to economic cycles.

Take a look at Marriott's operating model over the years, and you might say the company has evolved from a hotel company to an operations company, and now to a "branding and loyalty" company. Arne Sorenson and team believe the opportunity today is to partner with customers as they plan—and dream about—travel, creating a more intimate relationship with them while providing vastly more choices when they're away from home. Much of the emphasis since the Starwood acquisition has centered on creating this closer relationship with customers, embedding the brand in a continuous and customized engagement through its customer insights and loyalty programs. Among other changes, the company has now merged three loyalty programs (Marriott Rewards, Starwood Preferred Guest, and Ritz-Carlton Rewards) into a single unified platform called Bonvoy to engage with customers.

The integration of processes, structures, and technologies that underpin these capabilities are critical to Marriott's execution. Shannon Patterson, who has responsibility for connecting and managing Marriott's twenty-four customer engagement centers around the globe, described it this way: "The rewards program is an enabler. Part of the power of Marriott is that [the loyalty platform] runs underneath commercial services, reservations and distribution, and operations.

Especially as we evolve to a branding focus, we'll use the rewards and loyalty platform as an integrator to power these other capabilities. It's a key piece of the evolution here at Marriott over the past couple years."

To execute well, Marriott continues to clarify its operating model and refine the organization architecture around achieving a step-change in capability to build customer engagement. As Sorenson reminded us, if all the Starwood acquisition did was create a bigger hotel chain, Marriott would be disappointed. "That's not enough. How do customers benefit? That's the extra."

Where Are Your Best Bets to Excel?

The Marriott example illustrates the importance of continually refining and evolving your operating model to stay up with—or ahead of—changing customer expectations. Your operating model will help you identify and chart capabilities that are particularly strong and need to be leveraged. And it also reveals those areas where your organization may be vulnerable and needs to be strengthened.

At times, the changes may be incremental, representing continuous improvement within your existing operating model. At other times, just getting better may not be enough. Like the Red Queen in Alice in Wonderland, who had to run very fast just to stay in the same place, incremental improvements that make you better may still leave you behind competitors. Getting ahead and not falling behind may require you to innovate your operating model, investing in new capabilities and a new value proposition to achieve a step change in performance. And executional excellence may require charting your course in advance so that you can invest ahead of the curve.[9]

UPS: Turbocharge your strategic capability. David Abney recently described UPS strategy as providing customers with "advanced logistics solutions made possible by a broad portfolio of differentiated services and capabilities expertly assembled and integrated into our customers' businesses."[10] In recent years, the company's portfolio of services and capabilities has grown exponentially. As Theron Colvin, UPS strategy manager, described it,

Thirty years ago, we were a very simple company that was operating with high repetition, very refined processes, all streamlined toward operational efficiency. That was the company. Over the years, the company has become immeasurably more complicated. Not only have we gone to different geographies, but we've expanded our services. What started as two basic products and services has grown to more than 350 capabilities. And we stitch them together in millions of different ways for our customers, which makes today's business extraordinarily complex.

Because UPS runs one of the most sophisticated logistics operations in the world, it not only needs to deal with the scale and complexities of running its own network, but it also needs to incorporate the nuances of many different companies' logistics networks, each with their own specific needs. As Colvin put it, "We are dealing with everyone else's complexities along with our own."

The task can be daunting. How does a company like UPS continue to execute well as it continues to raise the bar on operational capability? The company takes a disciplined approach in identifying key areas for investment to develop the most critical capabilities in its operating model. It could easily get sidetracked or diverted, but as David Abney noted, "Companies today must constantly assess everything they do to ensure they're keeping pace. UPS has been doing that and we will continue to optimize every element of our business." The following are a few of the key investment areas.

Integrated customer solutions. Dealing with the complexity in UPS's customer base requires a capacity for customization. Creating integrated customer solutions is one of its biggest executional challenges, so the company has invested in more than 1,500 industry and supply chain experts who help customers analyze their supply chains and, in many instances, rethink their approach to logistics. Given its operational bent, UPS has formulated a repeatable process that helps customers identify areas for improvement, quantify the value to the business, and execute the changes. Its solutions often require multiple services and modes of transport (e.g., freight, logistics, express, etc.), so the company also has been enhancing its "One UPS" capability to make the whole process seamless for customers. As Alan Gershenhorn put it, "We white board with them to help them stop thinking in terms of forwarding, package, distribution, etc. but thinking in terms of their value chain and what they're trying to accomplish and then overlay the necessary capabilities."

Targeted industries. To distinguish itself, UPS has been concentrating on the toughest supply chain challenges in the most demanding industries. Although it serves customers across a broad array of sectors, UPS has been focusing on four: healthcare, tech, retail, and industrial manufacturing. Why? Put simply, sophisticated customers need sophisticated solutions, and UPS is doubling down on building expertise in industries that benefit most from UPS's global network, technologies, and portfolio of services.

E-commerce. The shift to online commerce is both exhilarating and accelerating. Just as it has changed consumer expectations, ecommerce has also changed procurement and customer expectations in the industrial world. UPS has invested in a multiyear journey to "lean into the future growth" of e-commerce, serving retailers, manufacturers, and the many other businesses looking to build direct distribution channels.

Global markets and trade. Abney is quick to point out that although e-commerce grabs much of the headlines, international markets remain the company's best long-term opportunity. Investing in infrastructure is vital if UPS is to continue its pace of international growth. As we've noted throughout the book, expanding its global network puts a strain on UPS's operating model. Its core customers increasingly need to ship globally as new markets emerge, grow, and connect with each other. To keep pace, UPS continues to expand its cross-border network of facilities, equipment, and infrastructure to more than 220 countries. Scope and flexibility are key as the company employs a variety of business models including outside service providers, agents, acquisitions, partnerships, and the like that give customers access to global markets.

Integrated technologies. Finally, technology serves as the backbone of UPS's operating model and organizational architecture. To transform and grow, UPS must continually innovate using advanced technologies and more data to drive sophisticated processes and faster decision making. Executives in the company repeatedly told us that in many cases, information is as important as the shipment itself, which is why visibility and control provided by UPS systems are essential to shippers and receivers. As Gershenhorn reminded us, "We're a technology company. That's how we need to be thinking because the technology and the business processes that are running your model, your network, your platform are where the true value is." UPS invests in excess of $1 billion a year in both customer-facing technologies (software that provides customers better visibility and control of their shipments) and operational technologies that automate and optimize internal processes and decision making. Of course, the goal is to develop a virtuous cycle of innovation: As UPS analyzes customers' supply chains and builds customized solutions for their toughest challenges, their systems capture data and new insights that lead to continuous learning and process improvement from each situation. The results are a deeper knowledge of the customer, a higher level of performance, and a capability that others can't easily replicate.

A couple of things to note about UPS's efforts to turbocharge its operating model: First, the investments fuel better execution by focusing on key value-added services that customers need/want most. So even as the company's portfolio increases in complexity, there is clarity about what matters most. Second, UPS's investments aren't single purpose or isolated to a particular part of the business; they can be leveraged across its entire portfolio of services. As Gershenhorn described it, "One of the big opportunities we have is to build offerings that combine the capabilities of all these business units to create something more powerful than the sum of the parts." That not only improves return on investment but it also strengthens the operating model because it combines investments in people, processes, and technologies that underlie the entire organization architecture.

Before moving on, there are a couple other points worth emphasizing about the Marriott and UPS examples. Each example illustrates the idea that in complex organizations you need to clarify your operating model first as a foundation for prioritizing key elements of execution.

But they also convey the idea that your operating model may need to evolve over time—or change dramatically—as the relationship between customer value and capabilities changes. To perform well, the organization architecture needs to be adjusted to support these changes, too. As we've noted, when the adjustments are not done, execution falters.

STREAMLINE YOUR ARCHITECTURE

After clarifying your operating model, you have a workable blueprint for refining your architecture to bridge strategy and performance. But "structure follows strategy" doesn't just happen automatically. There are two underlying causes for a mismatch of your organization architecture.

First, too often organizations are de facto designed to do yesterday's work. What does that mean? Over time, when companies go after emerging opportunities, their strategy morphs but they frequently don't adjust their architecture in concert. Structures, processes, and systems are notoriously intractable and stay in place while the organization goes after new opportunities. So while the strategy has adapted, the architecture hasn't.

To cope with the mismatch, managers devise workarounds or administrative add-ons that address problems in the short run (perhaps) but don't provide the fundamental fix required. In time, the organization grows in complexity and the architecture may no longer be appropriate. As UPS's Jim Barber put it, "As you're growing and finding success, you always should challenge yourself by asking, 'What's the next architecture?' Our architecture that was set up probably twenty years ago had matured to a place where it had us handcuffed. And if we didn't change the architecture, we'd never grow."

The second cause for a strategy-architecture mismatch is that companies adjust their structures reactively without using the operating model as a blueprint for change. Companies with performance problems often reorganize, addressing the symptoms of poor performance modifying reporting relationships, altering decision authority, perhaps even adhering to generally good advice about best practices. But if the changes don't address the underlying root cause of performance, the design choices may not be appropriate. And if the architecture isn't appropriate, managers will continue to devise quick fixes, duplicating effort, adding back layers, increasing complexity, and bureaucracy comes creeping back. This leads to vexing problems as the organization becomes increasingly unwieldy.

Not surprisingly, a Bain study found that when companies cease to create value and performance declines, the vast majority of CEOs (85 percent) blamed the problem on internal factors such as complexity, resources, and lack of focus.[11]

What's the solution? As we go through the next section, ask yourself these questions:

- Have we streamlined the organization structure to enable the key drivers of customer value?
- Are roles and responsibilities well defined, with clear decision rights and authorities?
- Have we created lateral connections across our structures to improve collaboration and joint decision making?

Can You Make It Simpler, Cleaner, Flatter?

One of our colleagues is fond of saying, "The two biggest deterrents to growth and success are . . . growth and success." Ironic, but true. As businesses excel, success reinforces existing ways of doing things and the natural tendency to obviate change. And in the context of organization architecture, growth and success also lead to increased complexity. Successful businesses inevitably expand their reach, scope, and scale, resulting in a larger, more sophisticated business. That complexity leads to a host of coordination problems, which can entangle performance and constrain further growth. The experiences of Microsoft, Marriott, UPS, and others all show us that growth, globalization, technology disruption, digital connectivity, and the like all compound the complexities of the organizational architectures.

Complexity begets complexity. And complexity is the enemy of execution. Amy Kates and Greg Kesler argued, "Excess hierarchical layers and duplicated work make the organization slow and internally focused."[12] The bloated organization also increases costs and inefficiencies.

Overly complicated structures, inefficient processes, and weak account-abilities are more likely to increase power struggles, communication gaps, and fractionalized work. Execution suffers.

So what's the solution? You can make progress in managing com-plexity by doing three things. First, identify those intersections where decisions, resources flows, and accountabilities get held up. As we noted at the outset of this chapter, these tend to proliferate in the gaps be-tween organizational units where collaborative work needs to happen but doesn't. Streamline the organization to make the bridges easier to cross. Simplify decision-making processes by clarifying roles and re-sponsibilities, establishing decision rights, and making accountabilities explicit. Doing so at these particular points is especially important. Take a minute to think, where are these in your organization?

Second, determine which processes are most visible to customers and critical for delivering on your value proposition. There may be literally thousands of processes in your organization—but which few are most critical? Here again, your operating model serves as a blueprint. Stream-lining these processes will go a long way toward helping the organization operate more efficiently, increasing speed to market, reducing defects and rework, increasing the quality of output, eliminating waste, and reducing cost. The good news is that when you streamline your core processes, you deliver better for customers and decrease costs at the same time.

Third, flatten your structure as much as possible, eliminating super-fluous hierarchy. We frequently hear executives talk about their latest "spans and layers" initiatives. One study found that while an average business has 8–9 layers, best-in-class companies try to limit the number to 7. Similarly, while the average span of control runs around 6–7 direct reports, the best-in-class companies extend to around 10–15.[13] But the search for such a magical number probably misses the point. The key is to assiduously push to eliminate layers that are not value-adding, and expand the scope of leadership to empower employees.

Other things being equal, minimizing complexity in these three spots helps improve decision making, resource sharing, and coordina-tion. Like Occam's razor and the principle of parsimony, the simplest solution in organization design is often the best.[14]

As the example from SunTrust illustrates below, perhaps the most important principle is to build an architecture that supports the critical priorities of your strategy. What we've learned from executives in our research is that they work to protect their core from the proliferation of complexities, to simplify work flows and line of sight to customers.

SunTrust: Design around key value drivers. Early in Bill Rogers's tenure as CEO, he identified a new architectural design to improve its execution capability. Even though SunTrust had undertaken major re-source reductions in 2010, the bank needed to improve its targeted efficiency ratio.

Under the company's old geographic structure in 2011, many of Rogers's direct reports were independent area heads overseeing all operations in their regions, ranging from the retail banking businesses to commercial and business banking. In other words, they had big, diverse portfolios and lots of autonomy. These leaders each had their own support infrastructure and dedicated marketing, finance, and HR functions. The structure was in part based on the legacy of prior acquisitions, and while it had worked in the past, it became suboptimal for the bank's revenue potential and cost position. It also limited cross-company coordination and enterprise-wide alignment.

Rogers's team saw an opportunity to improve clarity, efficiency, and ultimately, effectiveness, by shifting the organizational structure from a geographically led to a business unit- or segment-led model. As Mark Chancy explained: "Two years in as CEO, Bill made the second of what was a critical set of alignment decisions, which was to break down that geographic organizational structure by putting the retail branches into the Consumer segment and the Commercial Banking leadership and teams into the Wholesale segment. That allowed for complete realignment of what was happening in the field."

It also simplified the architecture. The company migrated to three business segments in 2012: Wholesale Banking, Consumer Banking and Private Wealth Management, and Mortgage Banking. Further in 2017, SunTrust aligned its Mortgage business within the Consumer Segment. Instead of regional presidents making strategic decisions regarding all types of business in their geographies, the segment leadership teams directed and coordinated the strategy across geographies.

The changes didn't stop there. As the bank went through its structural change, it also took a hard look at its core processes and systems. To streamline operations and clarify best practice, SunTrust mapped out, evaluated, and subsequently reengineered several of its core business processes. It became obvious during this same time period that SunTrust's technology architecture needed a boost. Underinvestment during the financial crisis made this the opportune time to update and integrate the IT infrastructure, and to do so to complement key processes and capabilities. Investments were evaluated by their ability to improve client experience, increase productivity, reduce operating costs, and enhance revenue. By making the IT and process changes at the same time SunTrust was restructuring, the team was able to simultaneously identify appropriate staffing levels within the new operating model. In so doing, they discovered opportunities to increase efficiency by redeploying human capital expense to areas of greatest need.

The new organizational architecture complemented the strategy that Rogers put in place to diversify the business mix and invest in growth opportunities, improve efficiency, and increase shareholder returns. It also provided a number of other benefits. First, it delivered an improved experience and value to clients. Also, investments in geography-agnostic industry specialists augmented the capabilities of local commercial relationship managers, allowing SunTrust to bring clients the broadest and most relevant solution set available.

Second, the new architecture ultimately resulted in a smaller chassis for the bank. One of the drivers of efficiency was the move of support services such as human resources and finance out of the fragmented structure in which they were organized and dedicated to a single region. Centralizing these functions unlocked cost savings through scale benefits, while also improving capability and the quality of services provided.

Finally, the new architecture accelerated the path to building alignment. The segments translated corporate strategy into goals and plans that were coordinated across geographies, while the lines of business began to break down silo walls and operate in an integrated way with a shared purpose and principles. As Chancy noted, "Our ability to influence, engage, and align strategy across product, process and technology initiatives was impeded by not having that alignment."

Organize One Way and Manage the Other

The SunTrust experience provides some important lessons about reconfiguring the organization in order to streamline operations and clarifying authority structures in order to create more value enterprise wide. There are inevitable tradeoffs, of course, and Rogers and team would readily acknowledge that there is no perfect solution. They emphasized the importance of designing an approach that was best for the company *at the time*, and to always be aware of what's coming next.

One of the safeguards we recommend is to "organize one way and manage the other." In other words, as senior executives make design choices, they should acknowledge the inherent tensions and tradeoffs, make them explicit, and attend to the structural gaps they create as well as those they fill. So for example, if your architecture gives more authority to lines of business, the way SunTrust did, you would be well advised to stay close to the needs of geographic regions and manage those explicitly.

To some degree, most any large organization lives within a matrix of business units, geographies, and functions. As Marriott's David Rodriguez told us, "You don't choose whether you have a matrix or not in your organization. Saying that you're in a matrix environment is just recognizing the fact that people have multiple influences on them all the time. The only choice you really have is to recognize those relationships exist, and then decide how you're going to manage them."

Let's look at the experience of Microsoft and how they balance competing organizational needs.

Microsoft: Create "one" enterprise. Satya Nadella inherited an organization from his predecessor, Steve Ballmer, that had been reorganized eleven times during his tenure. Some observed that it had almost become an annual ritual. However, Ballmer's last reorg—dubbed "One Microsoft"—was dramatic and fundamentally shifted the architectural design of the company to enable better collaboration and agility around common goals within Microsoft necessary to "enable innovation at a greater speed."

For prior decades, the company had been organized around separate product groups, each operating with relative autonomy to respond to their respective markets. But that led to an overly fragmented face to customers and to some unintended competition within the organization. In order to strive for success, Microsoft needed "better execution from product conceptualization and innovation right through to marketing and sales." The One Microsoft initiative was an effort to reinvigorate collaboration, break down barriers and silos, and really execute as a team. As Ballmer described it in a memo to all employees: "We are rallying behind a single strategy as one company—not a collection of divisional strategies. . . . We will see our product line holistically, not as a set of islands. We will allocate resources and build devices and services that provide compelling, integrated experiences across the many screens in our lives."[15]

Microsoft restructured from a product organization to a functional organization, joining together teams within engineering, business development, research, marketing, finance, human resources, legal, and operations. Within this structure, engineering had four subgroups that led the four key areas of the newly envisioned "devices and services" company: operating systems, applications, cloud, and devices. (These groups replaced eight separate product teams.) Each major initiative within Microsoft had a champion who organized to drive a cross-company team for success, integrating these different areas with the whole staff committed to the initiative's success.

It is easy to see the logic: each function had to coordinate with adjacent functions if it wanted its hard work to pay off and go to market. When Nadella became CEO, he retained this new structure, only making a few tweaks and some personnel changes but leaving the fundamental architecture in place. One Microsoft as a key initiative was dedicated to the idea of working across business units to achieve the company's mission.

To galvanize the approach, Nadella recruited company founder Bill Gates to spend time focusing on products and technology. Nadella's instinct was that no one had as much influence as Bill Gates within Microsoft, and he could be instrumental in ensuring collaboration among the different teams on projects of strategic product or technology development.

Still, the process hasn't necessarily been easy. As one executive observed, "One Microsoft is working to overcome years of a legacy where we had strong decentralization and strong organic divisions. Some would argue we took that too far, and there was a fear of certain groups even competing with each other. [In our new way of working], this is saying any solution or service that we have has to have One Microsoft and an end-to-end solution for the customer's benefit."

In the end, the company's performance breakthrough owes to three big effects of One Microsoft: focusing the whole company on a single integrated strategy, improving its capability in all functions and engineering/technology areas, and working more collaboratively around common goals.

What's the takeaway from the restructuring experiences of SunTrust and Microsoft? First, as much as possible, simplify your structures to clarify authority and decision rights in a way that aligns with the key value drivers of the business. Too many layers, too many divisions, too many gaps confound decision making and obscure line of sight to customers. Overly elaborate structures result in conflicting priorities, duplicate communication flows, and slow decisions.

Second, create an organizational latticework that enables collaboration across the formal structures. These can include cross-functional teams, joint committees, communities of practice, collective rewards, and shared governance. As we noted earlier, some elements of the architecture are hard-wired, while others are soft-wired. Both are important.

Finally, organize one way and manage the other. Be mindful of the power and gravitational pull of the formal organization architecture. Structure conveys authority, channels information, funnels resources, and creates power differentials that need to be managed with a personal touch. Executives and managers can be a countervailing force that balances the organizations and keeps design tradeoffs from disrupting the organizational equilibrium.

In the end, your organizational architecture has to manage two opposing forces. It needs to create separations that provide autonomy and authority so your people can accomplish their most critical tasks unencumbered. And then it simultaneously needs to create mechanisms for facilitating communication, coordination, and joint decision making that bind the organization back together. Long, long ago, Lawrence and Lorsch referred to these as structural differentiation and integration.[16] Both are necessary, and the more complicated your organization environment, the more of each you will need. More differentiation requires more integration. The trick is to do it in the most simple and uncomplicated way possible.

BUILD AN INTELLIGENT ARCHITECTURE

Let's pause for a second. There's a lot here to take in. So far in the chapter, we've emphasized the importance of clarifying your operating model as a blueprint for organization architecture. Doing so helps you focus on the main drivers of value, and the structures, processes, systems, and skills that underlie your core capabilities. In a complicated world, that exercise will help you identify the most important priorities for strategy execution and begin the process of designing an infrastructure that supports it.

Then we emphasized efforts to streamline your organization to resist the forces of complexity, to get noise out of the system, and avoid confusion that impedes decision making. Every design has tradeoffs, and the key is to configure the organization in a way that channels information and resources most efficiently, while preserving enterprise collaboration.

Now we'll go one step further: A well-designed architecture can also facilitate strategy execution by channeling data and information to inform better decisions. It all depends on the way you design your processes and information systems.

Let's start with processes. We can think of good processes as valuable "recipes" for doing work, repeatable and scalable sequences of actions that help streamline workflows. A whole cottage industry has arisen around the principles of process improvement and execution. We would not try to duplicate that here, but rather only acknowledge the value of interventions such as lean six sigma and business process reengineering to help us eliminate variance, reduce waste (aka "muda"), improve quality, and enhance productivity. UPS's success and reformulation of package delivery owes to doing just that. Similarly, SunTrust's breakthrough performance—with five consecutive years of earnings growth, tangible efficiency improvement, and increased shareholder returns—came from a fixation on purpose and performance with lean operations, delayering, and eliminating waste. At a minimum, execution is improved when processes and standard work are clearly defined, process owners are known and accountable, and measurement systems are used as a basis for decision making.

Information technology also matters. We can think of it euphemistically as providing blood flow through the anatomy of process improvement. Data and processes are complementary assets and increasingly inseparable. Even a good process without good information is an empty vessel, hollow and ineffectual. Technology investment without process improvement is, as they say, merely "paving cow-paths," reinforcing that which is perhaps circuitous and inefficient.[17] It may come as no surprise that executives view information access, utilization, and knowledge management as the most important sources of potential productivity gains over the next decade.[18]

We have found that information technology has three principle effects on execution: operational, relational, and transformational. At an operational level, information systems help standardize data and automate lower-value transactional work, eliminating inefficiencies that cripple decision making. Is your organization one of those still stymied by databases that are incompatible and can't talk to one another? Relationally, technologies also connect people in real time, providing them with shared access to data and information and, more so, enabling synchronous collaboration and real-time knowledge-sharing opportunities. At their best, technologies can transform processes by reducing or eliminating the separation of time and distance, supporting decisions that are both better and faster. We would emphasize again that our colleagues often lament that systems are more typically used for reporting (up) than informing (down). Don't overlook that point. The key for execution is to balance the two to make information available for better decision making.

Change is coming rapidly, and we may have reached an inflection point. Consider the following questions for your own organization:

- What steps have we taken to streamline our core processes to improve workflow, increase productivity, and eliminate waste?
- How well have we made information accessible and knowledge shared throughout the organization?
- Do information systems inform and enable better decision making with timely data?

Does Your Architecture Inform and Enable?

Digital transformation is accelerating and creating a paradigm shift for strategy execution. Most executives realize—at least in principle—the potential to use technology to better calibrate value streams and analyze data to respond faster to changing demand and external disruptions. So-called smart operations is an emerging approach that marries continuous improvement with real-time data analytics to transform the organization architecture. Technology helps us achieve what process improvement alone may not. If overly optimized processes become inflexible, they can leave the organization in a productivity "vice" unable to rapidly adjust to change and adapt. Smart operations makes continuous improvement practices more powerful by acquiring data in real time, using advanced analytics and higher levels of process orchestration to weave together separate workflows and decision streams in a faster and more synchronized way.

Phew, that's a lot to consider. Let's look at a good example that shows what UPS has been learning about smart operations.

UPS: Point your employees in the right direction. There is perhaps no process more critical to UPS's operating model than ensuring the reliability and efficiency of the "last mile" of delivery—getting the package to the customer's loading dock or doorstep. UPS's history of process improvement and systems engineering have taken aim at driver procedures and decision making since the company's inception. As Chief Human Resources Officer Teri McClure reminded us, "We're very execution focused, very much process driven. That's how the company has grown over the years; execution around very defined and engineered processes. We job measure everything." As the joke goes, UPS has so compulsively mapped its processes that UPS trucks don't make left turns because they're too inefficient. It's no joke. UPS drivers assiduously avoid left turns because they go against traffic, take longer, burn more fuel while idling, and incur safety risks.

Beyond process optimization, we noted earlier in the chapter how strategic UPS has been in developing advanced technologies that enable better decisions. One of the places that UPS has focused its investment is in its proprietary "On-Road Integrated Optimization and Navigation" initiative, better known as ORION. Jack Levis, UPS's senior director of process management, and a team of engineers developed ORION to give drivers real-time intelligence about the nature of routes, traffic, customer requests, and the like (see Figure 5.2). The ORION software tells them the most efficient route to deliver their packages.

Consider the mind-boggling complexity of decisions inherent in route optimization. Each UPS driver makes an average of 120 stops per day. What's the best route connecting those stops? The number of alternatives is 6,689,502,913,449,135,000,000,000,000,000,000,000,000,00 0,000,000,000,000,000,000,000,000,000,000,000,000,000,000,000, 000,000,000,000,000,000,000,000,000,000,000,000,000,000,000,00 0,000,000,000,000,000,000,000,000,000,000,000,000,000,000,000, 000,000,000,000,000,000 (give or take). Talk about big data!

Ten years in the making, ORION has been reputed to be the world's largest operations research project. It uses package-level detail, customized online mapping data, fleet telematics, and advanced algorithms to take route optimization to a whole new level. It is a powerful on-board decision support for drivers, making their jobs potentially easier and benefiting customers in the process with faster and customized deliveries.

To be candid, driver reaction to ORION has been mixed. As Levis recalled, "The project was nearly killed in 2007, because it kept spitting out answers that we couldn't implement." In the early stages, while ORION gave the best mathematical result, it didn't give sufficient regard to the interests and experience of the driver. Some drivers found the experience to be initially frustrating, especially if they needed to relinquish autonomy—and particularly if they didn't understand ORION's logic. (For example, ORION might instruct them to deliver a package in one neighborhood in the morning, and then come back to that same neighborhood later in the day.) Telling a driver with years of experience that an algorithm knew a better way to run their route didn't go over well at first.

So Levis's team decided to change the approach and give drivers discretion and a challenge. In other words, "beat the computer" by combining ORION's insights with their own knowledge and experience. Now drivers see ORION more as a *coach*—giving advice and support for their decisions. But drivers are encouraged to use their own judgment.

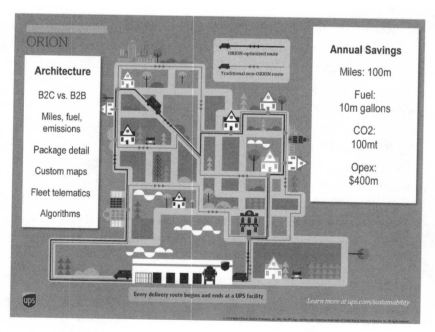

FIGURE 5.2 UPS Project ORION
Source: United Parcel Service of America, Inc. Reprinted with permission.

For example, if there is a traffic event that the system can't factor, drivers should override ORION (but document why). The goal is to create a mindset that a driver supported by ORION is the best of all worlds.

The system is paying off substantially. ORION reduces the total distance driven by 100 million miles annually, saving drivers precious time. It also helps get packages to customers sooner and generates more than $400 million in annual cost savings and avoidance. In addition, ORION has helped reduce fuel consumption by 10 million gallons, which cuts 100,000 metric tons of CO_2 a year (equivalent to taking 21,000 cars off the road). The net result? Better execution on several dimensions—customers are happy, employees are happy, shareholders are happy, and the planet is better off.[19]

What are the key takeaways from UPS's experience with ORION? Research from International Data Corporation shows that most companies are still relatively immature in their efforts to transform their operations. But progress is happening, and the pace is accelerating.[20] Still, most organizations are not in a position to match the sophistication of UPS's systems.

First, like other examples from companies in this chapter, the key for execution is to focus on your most critical drivers of performance. UPS focused on ORION because it was essential to "delivering" customer value. Find the most important processes and systems that support your core capabilities and make certain that the organization architecture is upgraded continuously to drive performance.

Second, what would drive better decisions? It's not data for data's sake, but data that informs better decisions. What information sources would lead to better and faster decisions? How can investment in better systems and analytics help here? Part of the value of machine learning is the capacity to support better decisions by humans and/or to automate the decisions. Again, the key to execution is better decisions faster.

Third, who needs to share that information, both to make better decisions and to orchestrate related processes in a multiplex value stream? At the end of the day, the complications we noted with regard to structure, processes, and systems need to be reconciled. The potential of sophisticated technologies will not automatically make these other challenges go away. So we would reiterate that the goal is to create an organization architecture that is well integrated across the enterprise and aligned with most important requirements of your operating model.

WHERE DO YOU STAND?

Just like in the previous chapters on Alignment and Ability, we hope you do two things at the end of this chapter. First, assess yourself on the key elements of Architecture in the checklist below (Table 5.1). But second, reflect on how each of the elements of the 4A framework interact and reinforce one another.

Take a few minutes to do a realistic self-assessment, using the questions above. Compare yourself to the examples we shared. In some cases, you may be ahead of the game. In places where you're behind, use the lessons learned by these companies to begin a dialogue with others in your organization about the challenges and opportunities with your organization architecture. Doing so will help you devise the first steps forward.

TABLE 5.1 Architecture Checklist

ARCHITECTURE CHECKLIST	
Clear Operating Model	1. We have clarified our operating model that connects core capability to our customer value proposition.
	2. For each capability, we know which processes, systems, structures, and skills are most critical.
	3. We have prioritized key areas for investment to enhance our capability system for the future.
Streamlined Organization	4. We have streamlined the organization structure to facilitate the key drivers of customer value.
	5. Roles and responsibilities are well defined with clear decision rights and authorities.
	6. We have created lateral connections across our structure to improve collaboration and joint decision making.
Intelligent Architecture	7. We have streamlined our core processes to improve workflow, increase productivity, and eliminate waste.
	8. Information is accessible and knowledge shared throughout the organization.
	9. Information systems inform and enable decision making with timely data.

© Scott A. Snell and Kenneth J. Carrig

Clarify Your Operating Model

In this chapter, we didn't simply note the importance of streamlining and clarifying your operating model; we gave you examples and approaches to consider. Your operating model depicts which capabilities are most vital for creating value and is a blueprint for designing and refining your organization architecture. This blueprint makes clear the key priorities for execution and shines a light on the structures, processes, systems, and skills that you may need to address first.

How clear is your operating model? Given the complexity of most organizations, a clear operating model is especially important to help focus your efforts. Also, that operating model helps you tie other elements of the 4A framework together. A clear articulation of your value proposition and capabilities is important for achieving alignment in the organization (Chapter 3), knowing which skills and talent pools are most critical (Chapter 4), and which elements of the architecture need to be reconfigured. The best companies are constantly reassessing their operating model to bring these elements together to drive execution.

Streamline Your Architecture

Laurence Peter, author of *The Peter Principle*, jokingly said, "Bureaucracy defends the status quo long past the time when the quo has lost its status."[21] If your architecture has become too complicated, it probably is slowing down decision making, disrupting collaboration, increasing inefficiencies, increasing costs, and stifling performance. Is this true? Not only does it make execution more difficult, it tends to create organization inertia that prevents rapid response and innovation. It's a common complaint.

So the question is, have you done the work necessary to streamline and simplify your architecture? As we noted at the beginning of the chapter, one of the most frequent obstacles to execution is "silos, slippage, and sludge." In this chapter, we laid out some guiding principles for streamlining your organization—clarifying roles and decision rights, eliminating unproductive layers and hierarchy, and clustering work together where collaboration directs line of sight to customers. As with our discussion of your operating model, the key is to home in on those elements that matter most and concentrate your investment there. The reality is that complexity won't go away, but a simplified architecture can help guard against the inefficiencies that complexity may bring. More importantly, it can facilitate decision making that clears the path for execution.

Build an Intelligent Architecture

Part of the challenge in designing your architecture is clarifying who has authority to make decisions. And part of the challenge is creating an intelligent architecture that channels information to those decision makers so they are more empowered. Advanced systems, data analytics, and other technologies are transforming the way work gets done and the capacity to make better and faster decisions. It is a disruptive force for sure, and represents a paradigm shift for operations and strategy execution.

Is your organization asking these questions?

- Why do we need further investment in technology?
- How will it change our ability to execute, creating new and better capabilities to deliver value?
- What specific decisions and actions would be improved along the way?
- Who needs to be involved?

World-class people, processes, systems, and structures underlie your core capabilities. That's the essence of organizational architecture.

WHAT'S NEXT? GET NIMBLE: AGILITY

As we've worked our way through the 4A framework, it's perhaps become more obvious how Alignment, Agility, and Architecture are interconnected. Each plays a unique role in supporting execution capability, and they complement one another in building a mutually reinforcing system. In the next chapter, we address the requirements of Agility—the responsiveness of the organization, its ability to shift rapidly to change, and the capacity to learn, innovate, and thrive in a world of disruption.

while simultaneously investing in its capacity to adapt and respond organizationally.

We've joked with Rob Katz and his team at Vail Resorts that organizational agility is a lot like skiing moguls. And the first rule of skiing moguls is to keep your head level and your chest pointed downhill toward your goal. Anyone who takes on each mogul one at a time, wrenching their whole body back and forth to approach one bump after another, will become unbalanced and probably fall. But by maintaining a level head with constant orientation toward the goal, and then flexing from the waist down, the skier has a better chance. "And you've got to be three turns ahead," Katz reminded us.

The analogy to organizations isn't far off. Agility requires a clear direction and strong core, while simultaneously building flexible behaviors and capabilities. Indeed a recent McKinsey study suggests that what makes agile companies special is their ability to do both.[8]

As we discuss the ways that you can build flexibility and responsiveness in your organization, we'll also reinforce many of the lessons from our chapter on Alignment. Articulating a clear strategic intent, purpose, and identity; building shared expectations for high performance; and instilling a culture of mutual accountability help you to maintain the critical orientation of the organization while simultaneously building the capacity for change. Alignment is not only complementary to agile execution; it may be indispensable for it.

But don't miss the bigger point here. Alignment is necessary, but insufficient for agile execution. As we noted at the beginning of the chapter, alignment alone can facilitate execution in the short run, but blind the organization and stifle needed change. Alignment AND the capacity for adaptation is the key to agility.

DEVELOP SITUATIONAL AWARENESS

In working with the U.S. military, it has been interesting to observe how frequently they refer to "situational awareness" as a prerequisite for agile execution. The term is used by military personnel and others working in dangerous occupations to convey the importance of staying alert to your surroundings for potential changes in the environment. The relevance of the concept extends to decision making in other areas as well. In complex and dynamic environments, we need to be aware of how elements and events are in play, interacting, reshaping context, and how our actions may be impacted as a result.

Sometimes situational awareness involves paying attention to faint signals, small cues that portend larger events, much the way an increase or decrease in building permits is a leading indicator of a bigger shift in the macroeconomy. But situational awareness goes beyond simply being "aware" of what's happening. It requires interpreting and understanding the implications of those interconnected events as well. Ultimately, situational awareness involves evaluating the importance or value of some information relative to others in order to project, anticipate, adjust, and—just maybe—influence future events.[9]

In the context of agile execution, we've learned that situational awareness is perhaps THE critical contingency variable that indicates whether an organization is proactive, versatile, and responsive, or reactive, scrambling, flailing—and failing—in crisis. As we go through this section, ask yourself these questions:

- How thoroughly do we learn about our customers in order to foster deeper relationships?
- How many points of contact have we created with external stakeholders to ensure relevance and responsiveness?
- How do we recognize faint signals to stay ahead of emerging trends?

How Well Do You Know Your Customers, Really?

Situational awareness is strongest among those with great experience, deep learning, and accumulated expertise. Wesley Cohen and Daniel Levinthal's concept of "absorptive capacity" builds on much of what we have described above in terms of a firm's ability to recognize and evaluate external information, assimilate it, and apply it in ways that improve its adaptive capabilities. Perhaps intuitively, the depth and breadth of a firm's prior related experience influences its ability to process new information and knowledge, and because of that, it is a prerequisite to further organizational learning.[10]

We focus here on deep knowledge of customers, not because they are the only stakeholder in an organization's environment, but because they are in many ways the most important. As we emphasized in the prior chapter on Architecture, customers are the focal point of the firm's operating model and the primary arbiter of value creation. At some level what applies to learning about customers is relevant to learning about other stakeholders as well, such as shareholders, employees, competitors, suppliers, regulators, NGOs, and so forth.

Let's take a look at what Vail Resorts has been doing to gain deep learning about its customers.

Vail Resorts: Mine big mountains of data. Recall that Rob Katz's goal is to transform the ski industry: not just to respond to what others are doing, but to drive change and innovation to which others must react. He and his team have been working to build a strong portfolio of resorts and invest in building organizational capability that is best in the world. He is passionate about changing the relationship with customers, changing the way they think about skiing, and changing the way they engage with Vail. To do that, Katz and his team knew they had a lot of homework to do, learning first about the people who do—and don't—ski at Vail Resorts.

Customer data. Like other organizations in other industries, Katz knew that Vail needed to mine the potential of big data, and doing so involved blending information technology, market research, and customer service. Vail launched Epic Pass, its new season pass that allowed customers to pay one price and ski any of the company's resorts around the world. Customers loved it.

As Katz sees it, "Epic Pass was an innovation where we were able to give our customers incredible value." But it also gave Vail much greater insight to their customers; *where* they skied (which resorts, which slopes, which lifts), *how* they skied (vertical descent, slope rating, frequency), and even *why* they skied (interests, lifestyle, demographics). Using a mobile app called EpicMix and RFID technology, customers could track their vertical feet, earn pins, share action photos, challenge friends, and connect via social media. Soon the data extended beyond just season pass holders to everyone who bought a ticket.

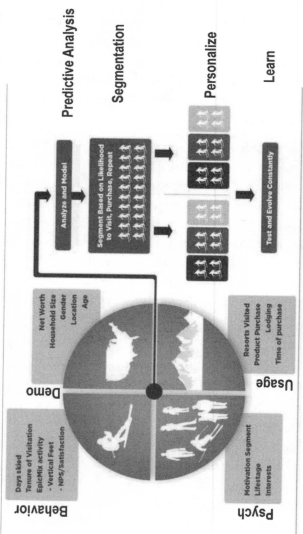

FIGURE 6.1 Vail Resorts Customer Analytics
Source: Vail Resorts, Inc. Reprinted with permission.

Generate insights. As shown in Figure 6.1, Vail Resorts developed best-in-class data capture that provided transparency into guest behavior. The company has a growing database of more than 14 million contractible guest records, giving them a chance to develop predictive analytics of the likelihood customers would visit, purchase, repeat, and so on. The company developed eighty distinct customer segments that allowed them to personalize communication to each customer. It has completely redefined customer engagement and loyalty.

Of course, the value of segmentation and personalization is that it leads to a richer more customized engagement (and repeat business). But Katz doesn't see it just as a tool for CRM and data-driven marketing, but more broadly as a foundation for deeper organizational learning and agility. The different resorts in Vail's portfolio can use the data to experiment a bit in a very controlled way, try out new ideas in different segments, test and evolve.

The lesson learned? The more you know, the more you can learn. And the more you'll be able to leverage that knowledge to create new ways of engaging customers. The Vail example really shows how deep learning goes far beyond simply gauging customer satisfaction. It involves getting to the foundation of what drives their decisions and behavior in order to gain better insights about what they might value, and how you can respond accordingly.

What's Living (and Dying) in Your Ecosystem?

It's not unusual for executives to begin drawing analogies to biology, ecology, and the natural environment when talking about their approach to organizational agility. And for good reason. They construe the challenges of agility not just as meeting customer needs but as attending to the larger context of a whole array of stakeholders in the broader environments. These include shareholders, suppliers, distributors, competitors, partners, and other diverse communities.

James F. Moore's concept of the business ecosystem captures this pretty well, where "organisms" compete, cooperate, exchange resources, and coevolve, establishing a fairly stable community of symbiotic relationships over time. Innovation, change, or disruption in one part of the system can reverberate throughout the entire ecosystem, leading to transformation, self-renewal, or sometimes even death. The challenge for leaders, those who establish prominent roles in the ecosystem, is to collaborate with others to bring new ideas, innovation, and a compelling vision of the current ecosystem, while competing against those who would threaten the system or innovate to create an alternative ecosystem.[11]

Ironically, a number of executives in our roundtables candidly admitted, given other dynamics in their industries, that they don't spend a lot of time worrying (just) about competitors. Not because competitors are unimportant, but because the action-response sequences with their rivals are fairly well established. More worrisome, they said, were the unknowns, myriad possible events and conditions that were hard to predict, difficult to untangle, and yet had far-reaching consequences. These executives had a clear sense that the rules were changing in their industries but not yet completely known. In that regard, agility for these companies was about building the versatility to influence the change and to thrive in a variety of future environments, not just the current one.

Marriott: Evolve the ecosystem. Marriott has recognized changes occurring in its ecosystem, and the possibility for disruption by online travel agencies (OTA), aggregators, and other hospitality platforms. But rather than resist changes in the ecosystem, Sorenson and team are working to understand the dynamics, the potential benefits to customers, and the ways in which Marriott can lead.

As he described the challenge: "With 30 brands and 6,000 hotels in 120 countries and loyalty programs, how do you create an ecosystem of customers that basically say 'I really don't need to go anywhere else? I don't need to go to Expedia. I don't need to go to Hilton. I don't need to go to Airbnb because no matter where I'm going, you're going to have a range of choices for me, and I know you're going to take care of me.'"

Customer centric. How has Marriott been working to evolve that ecosystem? Like the Vail Resorts story above, Marriott keeps the interests and loyalty of its customer front and center. Adam Malamut, Marriott's chief customer experience officer, noted, "Everything we do is oriented around deep customer knowledge and intelligence. That is where it all starts. If you understand your customer needs today and have a mechanism by which you are also exploring what their needs might be in the future, that should always be your true north."

Self-disrupt. Looking to the future, Marriott is actually disrupting its own business model: "Organizations find their demise when they're hyperfocused on operating the business model that got them to where they are versus creating mechanisms strategically to disrupt that business model and open up the mindset around what could be."

Identify emerging trends. To open up to new possibilities, Marriott is generating lots of data about the external world. Some of it is traditional customer survey data. But increasingly the company is looking for emergent patterns across diverse sets of unstructured data sources. Malamut's team leverages external networks for accelerating new ideas and trends that could change the business:

> My Innovation Team and my Insight Team do a lot of exploration, and partnerships, and codiscovery with other companies around what they're doing. Because all of that becomes very valuable information that we could apply to transform our business in a noninsular way. We spend a lot of time every year thinking about emerging trends and disruptions to society, economies, etc., be it technology or regulations, whatever it might be, and that is a very powerful insight generation.

Use broad external networks. Some of these external networks include peers in the hotel business, and they are important because they are part of Marriott's immediate ecosystem. But many are not. The company learns from a wide array of firms; tech startups, retail and service entities, consultants, and futurists. Marriott recently established a joint venture with e-commerce giant Alibaba to engage Chinese customers in a different way, bring them into their loyalty program, and develop more insights into that market.

Evolve. Where is it all heading? That's confidential. And maybe a little bit unknown. But Malamut suggests that Marriott sees the travel ecosystem evolving as the "nexus of design, technology, and the human touch." In terms of design, Marriott sees its potential role as a partner across the whole travel journey, from unique locations to customized experiences, to special events—not just nice hotels. Its new "Marriott Moments" is an online portal where the company curates and designs possible travel experiences with customers. "The connective tissue is the data we know about our customers so that we can personalize each of those moments."

According to CEO Sorenson, "To bring that ecosystem to life also means you do not just have a transactional relationship with your hotel guest, but you have a travel relationship with them where they are communicating with us about what they dream of for travel and where they are co-creating with us." And Marriott is steadfast in its belief that its staff is still the key differentiator around the world, building an emotional connection with its customers. As the ecosystem evolves, Marriott is learning to adapt and flex with its customers, bringing more opportunities and reinforcing its role as a trusted partner.

Marriott's experience reinforces three key elements that are foundational for agility. First, the company has resolved to evolve its relationships with customers, a point that we highlighted in the chapter on Architecture, enhancing its value proposition and capability sets that support it. Second, this example reflects the reality that the broader ecosystem is evolving as well, and Marriott is careful not only to stay abreast of those changes but to help influence them. Instead of being disrupted by new channels and technologies, it is leading the charge. Third, Marriott's experience reveals the importance of keeping focused while undergoing change. Although Sorenson team is adapting to the current environment, it has not changed its essential culture of customer-centricity and purpose.

Peripheral Vision: Can You See in All Directions?

To this point we've discussed the importance of developing deep customer knowledge and a thorough understanding of the evolving ecosystem. One of the other keys to agile execution—and encompassed within the general frame of situational awareness—is improving your peripheral vision; that is, being cognizant of events on the margins that may not (yet) be in clear focus. There is very strong evidence that innovation occurs at the boundaries within and between organizations. So does disruption. And the more diverse the ecosystem, the more important it is to manage these broad interfaces.

In their book, *Peripheral Vision*, George Day and Paul Schoemaker reinforced the idea that opportunities and threats begin as weak signals from these boundary areas. And their research shows that less than 20 percent of firms have developed the capacity to be sufficiently vigilant and constantly attuned. They argue that organizations can develop early warning systems by doing five things: (1) scoping widely enough to ask the right questions, (2) scanning actively in the right places, (3) interpreting what the signals mean, (4) probing carefully for more information, and (5) acting wisely on signals before others do. Let's look at how these take shape at UPS.[12]

UPS: Look both ways. Given the complexity of UPS's business model, the broad set of technical capabilities it employs, and the variety of industries from which its customers come, it may not be surprising to learn that one of the company's chief agility challenges is staying up on what's coming in the future.

The company needs to look down the road, and look both ways. As Alan Gershenhorn put it, "There's just so much opportunity out there, and while we're very technologically advanced, our people get consumed in the near term. With all the greatest ambition and intent, you want to look out long term. But you quickly get gobbled up with all the short-term opportunity, and so your vision becomes very nearsighted."

UPS has taken some distinct steps to improve environmental scanning and engagement.

Scope broadly. First, the company scopes broadly, participating in a wide range of governmental exchanges, NGOs, and industry associations. For example, UPS is a strategic partner with the World Economic Forum based in Switzerland that convenes over 2,500 top business leaders, international political leaders, and economists to discuss the most pressing issues facing the world. Apart from UPS's immediate interests

in facilitating international trade, the company benefits by being involved in broader conversations about economic development, science
and technology, sustainability, and the like.

Scan and interpret constantly. Second, the company's business model
gives it a wide-angle lens to different industries. As Gershenhorn noted,
"One of our big advantages is the breadth and depth of our customer
base, from startups to the multinationals. Spending time with them, we
have a purview into everybody's value chain and what they're working
on. That's also a tremendous source of opportunity." UPS has developed
a program where senior executives are attached to various companies as
relationship managers, providing a two-way exchange of knowledge and
information. It is also a way to improve the company's signal detection,
early signs of change in the environment.

Probe the future. Third, like other companies, UPS has created a
Strategic Enterprise Fund to take a small stake in promising startup
ventures that focus on products, services, and technologies that may reshape industries. As shown in Figure 6.2, the portfolio has evolved over
time, but helps UPS collaborate with and learn from companies actively
developing new business models, promising market spaces, and emerging technologies. As Gershenhorn put it, "We can help them, and they
can help us."

Delve deeply. Finally, UPS has created some specialized units, Skunk
Works of sorts, which are concentrated areas of expertise given the autonomy and resources—away from the confines of day-to-day operations, to probe more deeply into areas that are of special importance to
the company. For example, because emerging B2C market opportunities
are so critical and evolving, UPS created a special Global E-commerce
Group that operates "almost a shadow strategy group whose whole role
is just to focus on that." Similarly, the company recently announced the
creation of the Advance Technology group, and specialized groups in
key industry sectors such as health care.

The rationale is to combine the power of broad environmental scanning with the leverage of deeper strategic investigation. As Gershenhorn

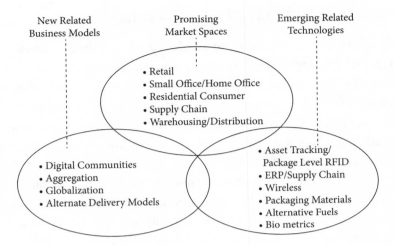

New Related
Business Models

Promising
Market Spaces

Emerging Related
Technologies

- Retail
- Small Office/Home Office
- Residential Consumer
- Supply Chain
- Warehousing/Distribution

- Digital Communities
- Aggregation
- Globalization
- Alternate Delivery Models

- Asset Tracking/
  Package Level RFID
- ERP/Supply Chain
- Wireless
- Packaging Materials
- Alternative Fuels
- Bio metrics

FIGURE 6.2 UPS Strategic Enterprise Fund
Source: United Parcel Service of America, Inc. Reprinted with permission.

sees it, "Over the past twenty years, we've created a systematic scalable way to study the market, look for opportunities, understand the issues and then address them, whether it's through new capabilities, new solutions, or a change in the way we operate."

UPS, Marriott, and Vail give us a better understanding of the different ways organizations prepare themselves for agile execution. The key is to develop better situational awareness of what might happen, where possibilities exist, and how the organization can respond. First, deep knowledge of—and empathy for—customer needs and interests helps you focus not just on what customers want today, but what they might value in the future. Second, understanding of the business ecosystem helps you interpret and influence the dynamics of all the interrelated parties, how they are engaging with one another, and how stable interaction patterns might be shifting. Finally, peripheral vision is important to help you look for early signs that outlying events and trends may impact your business. All of these approaches are helpful, and together they will give you a more "heads-up" approach to agile execution with a better field of vision, more acuity, and better able to see what's coming.

EMPOWER ORGANIZATIONAL LEARNING

One of the important truths of agile execution is that organizations adapt better—and faster—by taking smaller steps, questioning and learning as they go, iterating with repeated tests of data, and validating their progress. The approach sits in contrast to strategy execution as a one-time megalaunch and is based on fundamentals of organizational learning: the notion that an organization improves its ability to adapt over time as it gains experience.

Agile companies place a premium on learning faster and translating that learning into action. What we used to know isn't nearly as important as what we need to know. So the capacity to gather, interpret, create, share, and apply new learning is the essence of agile execution.

Research suggests that there are four key requirements for organizational learning: (1) openness to the outside world (what we have already described as situational awareness), (2) employees are empowered to own and solve problems, (3) experimentation and small bets, and (4) sharing knowledge throughout the organization.[13]

As we go through this section, consider the following questions in terms of how well your organization does each:

- How well do we empower members of the organization to own and solve problems, distribute decision making lower in the organization, and gain from their collective knowledge?
- In what ways have we established the capacity to manage reasonable risk by trying new things, prototyping, testing, and learning?
- How well do we share what we've learned in one part of the organization with those in other parts?

How Can You Lower the Center of Gravity?

In order to improve their agility, athletes often try to create a lower center of gravity, distributing their weight in order to achieve better balance and leverage. The parallel to organizations is not hard to imagine. Lowering the center of gravity involves decentralizing authority, empowering decision making, distributing initiative and action, clarifying decision rights, and building means for horizontal collaboration.

The truth is that agile execution cannot be run solely from the C-suite. Senior leaders don't try to master mind and monitor all aspects of the organization and the environment on their own. Even if they could, response times in hierarchical organizations are too slow. Rather than overspecify the details, senior leaders provide guidance to help shape strategic initiatives as they emerge from within the organization.

In our chapter on Ability, we noted that executional excellence depends on building great talent and collaboration down through the organization. Agile firms take advantage of the ability—coupled with clear alignment—to empower the organization.

By lowering the center of gravity for decisions and strategic action, senior executives aren't just empowering others to act on the strategy, they are gaining more insight to what is occurring both inside and outside the organization. In their book, *The Agility Factor,* Worley, Williams, and Lawler argue that more points of contact with the environment provide potentially more useful information. They refer to this as maximizing the "surface area" of the organization to learn from the environment.[14]

Marriott has been taking a similar approach, and finding the payoffs to be significant.

Marriott: Learn and grow from the ground up. Arne Sorenson and team recognize the power of harnessing the collective knowledge and experience within its workforce to energize agility. And Marriott has been working to shift the model to better enable that potential. But it is not as easy as it sounds. "It's still arguably our biggest challenge," said Adam Malamut. "We are a hyper-consensus-driven organization and top down in a lot of ways. So we continuously try interventions to create degrees of freedom for employees to experiment and try things in different ways."

Empower the organization. Prior to the Starwood acquisition, Marriott had already been making strides. As Sorenson said, "We were really trying to ramp up the pace of innovation and change in the company, and that to me was mostly about telling people (a) it was important and (b) they had permission. It was not so much about directing, because we're blessed with lots and lots of great talent. 'OK, you got it. Go—go do it.'"

Does the rich heritage of Marriott perpetuate traditional ways of doing things that can inhibit agility? "Oh, absolutely it does," said Sorenson. "The heritage of a culture of execution can be a culture of never make a mistake." CHRO David Rodriguez added, "Yes, we're focused on execution, but even more so on results. That's why we've been able to move away from the past, when it became clear we'd better be more innovative if we want to stay at the top of this industry."

Experiment locally. One of the great assets for collective knowledge and innovation is Marriott's network of hotels. "We have sort of a living lab out there of six thousand operating tests," Sorenson said. "Each one is very much connected back to the platforms and the brands, but they're each independently operated businesses that are localized." By empowering those businesses, with local food, local beverages, local design, and learning from their experience, Marriott has an opportunity to "mine that living lab every day."

But the approach is not without risk. "There are a lot of things now that happen that I never green light," said Sorenson. "You still want people to do their homework and try and understand why [a new idea] is going to work, but you've got to let them experiment. You've got to let them move. Occasionally somebody is going to make a bone-headed move, and you can't beat them up for it because if you do, you've basically thrown a wrench right back into the whole thing." By giving the hotel staffs discretion to experiment and explore, Marriott fuels broader organizational learning. The variation in local approaches and ideas helps to create the potential for more organizational versatility. And that versatility is a foundation for agility.

Leverage the collaborative network. Another way Marriott learned to tap into the collective knowledge of its workforce is developing what it calls Talent Network Teams. The effort is designed to let employees own and solve problems by co-creating a communication network throughout the company and a reciprocal feedback mechanism to share knowledge. Here's how it works: A business leader sets up a challenge they're trying to resolve, and puts out a call to Marriott associates around the world to join a virtual project team to address the challenge, leverage the network, generate new ideas, and derive solutions. As Malumut describes it, the teams are "an incredible organizational learning mechanism where it's almost like small pods of internal incubation." The team charter is essentially "Break a mold, let's think of new solutions." Anyone can be involved from any discipline. "It's a really interesting cultural intervention to co-create with our staff," said Malamut. The added benefit, over and above the immediate problem solving and idea generation, is that the teams are also an informal development mechanism, representing real-time learning, the chance to build out a network, and learn from others in the business.

Seed new ideas. Finally, Marriott has been empowering new ideas and new ways of working through its investment in the "Travel Experience Incubator." In partnership with Accenture Interactive and 1776, an international business incubator, Marriott seeds startups that bring innovation to the travel industry. "This is a mechanism by which we can feed and curate startup companies that frankly are uninhibited by organizational prophecy," Malamut said. "Their whole mission is to discover something that is inextricably new that does not exist. The incubation, venturing, external networking approach is a structured external entrepreneurship type of model that feeds your business. It allows for a greater freedom and flexibility of idea generation and boldness that can feed back into your business in a more cost-effective way."

Add it all up, and we can see how Marriott has been building a broader base of idea generation, knowledge creation, and collaborative learning. The company has been getting better and better at bringing ideas from the field back to the center, and it's opening up new possibilities for innovation and agility.

Can You Learn Faster By Getting More Reps?

In the fitness world, there is an adage: "Heavy lifting leads only to size and bulk. If you want to improve agility, use lighter weights and do more reps." Organizations that "max out" and approach strategy execution only from the standpoint of resource optimization, scale-economies, and efficiency maximization tend to become big, single-purpose machines. Their efforts to attempt agile response involves major muscle movements that place a lot of strain on the organization. Truly agile organizations tend to make smaller investments, with more variety, spread out over more repetitions.

Instead of running pilots before big launches, more and more companies are moving in a very intentional way toward the agile principles of design thinking, prototyping, and proof of concept. As depicted in Figure 6.3, the change in mindset is getting the organization to let go of impatience to scale and replacing it with an understanding of the value of iterating on a smaller scale.

As Marriott's Malamut described it,

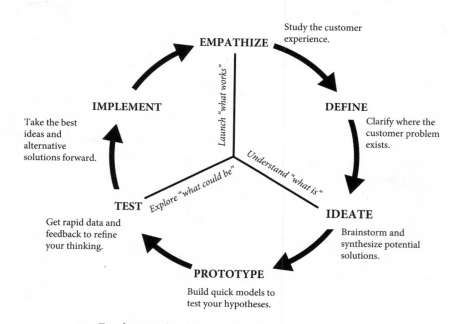

FIGURE 6.3 Fundamentals of Design Thinking
Adapted from: T. Brown, *Change by Design: How Design Thinking Transforms Organizations and Inspires Innovation* (New York: HarperCollins, 2009); B. Burnett and D. Evans, *Designing Your Life: How to Build a Well-lived, Joyful Life* (New York: Knopf, 2016); J. Liedtka and T. Ogilvie, *Designing for Growth: A Design Thinking Tool Kit for Managers* (New York: Columbia Business School, 2011).

We get things ready in great partnership with all stakeholders to move quickly and then experiment within the field, learn from it, and pivot. Within that process, failing early on is acceptable because dying before we try to go to scale is actually a good thing. I've been in instances where we didn't know enough before we spent our money and built it out to scale. We didn't spend enough time kicking the tires with the users of the product or directly with the customers.

The more of these experiments, the more iterations, the more learning, the more the organization begins to resemble a mosaic of possible alternative futures. Private equity firms, venture funds, biopharma, and other organizations often operate this way, where the expected return from any single investment may be lower, but the expected return of the overall portfolio of investments is very high.

The key is to learn quickly from these smaller bets. By collecting data, seeing what works and what doesn't, it is possible to test your assumptions about the market and make adjustments more quickly. Your management team needs to be aligned and ready to kill unpromising projects, and reallocate resources (money, talent, time, and other resources) to more promising alternatives.

Here's an example from Microsoft that shows how they are embracing agile principles.

Microsoft: Learn quickly and respond better. Microsoft has shifted the way it goes to market with new products, an approach that emphasizes rapid testing and learning. In the past, the company was guilty of what some called "launch and leave," meaning Microsoft would develop a product based on their own internal expertise, make a big launch to the market, and then move on to build the next thing. A successful product was one that sold well, yes, but the feedback cycle was very long, and often the company didn't have good data on how people used the product. So it was difficult to learn quickly.

Today, Microsoft has a different, more agile process. As Scott Guthrie, EVP of the Cloud and Enterprise Group, described it, "One thing that we have tried to change is how to get a minimum viable product or strategy that we think is right, use data, and then course correct." Instead of using revenue as the key data, Microsoft focuses on customer usage. "Revenue's a trailing indicator," said Guthrie. "Let's be agile, and let's be data driven. The first thing I do in the morning isn't check my revenue. I check the usage for each of my core businesses." Shorter feedback cycles, with faster accurate data, makes it easier to make adjustments. And since so much more is on the cloud, updates can be almost immediate. "It's infinitely easier to move one degree at a time, 365 days of the year, than it is to do one fell swoop."

Hypothesis testing. Microsoft's approach frames each iteration as a form of hypothesis testing and using data to test those hypotheses. "If something isn't working, what are the hypotheses for how we fix it? And then every time we try one of these hypotheses, did it actually move the needle?" Learning in that sense is both systematic and incremental.

Embrace a growth mindset. Satya Nadella has emphasized that agility begins with a growth mindset, and he places this front and center in virtually all of his communication about Microsoft's culture change. As CHRO Kathleen Hogan observed, "This notion of constantly being curious and learning and open to feedback, and you don't have all the answers, breeds agility. If you have that fixed mindset, where you feel you need to be the smartest person in the room, you have to have it all figured out." A growth mindset embraces ambiguity and acknowledges mistakes as an investment in learning.

Learn from mistakes. How open are people at Microsoft to really making a mistake? "I think this alone was probably the biggest shift in our company," said Chuck Edward, head of global talent. "We had a lot of smart, passionate people, but when you remove this fear of judgment or fear of mistakes and you allow people to try things, it was just cathartic." In the end, Guthrie emphasizes that agility and "growth mindset isn't about being right. There's no absolute, and if you think you're right, and you think you're perfect, that's a really dangerous place to be because the world's constantly changing."

Evolve the performance system. Not surprisingly, Microsoft is one of a growing number of companies rethinking its approach to performance management, and its rationale ties directly to principles of agility. In

2013, the company dramatically altered its performance review process, eliminating traditional ratings and forced rankings. Gone is the one-size-fits-all approach that had a fixed timeline for evaluations, usually annually: now managers are encouraged to give feedback when and where it makes sense given the cycles of the business. Goal setting has shifted as well. The new system replaces "commitments," which were personal goals like sales quota or customer retention, with "core priorities," which can include commitments but also incorporate how well an employee works as a team player.

Rather than a traditional stack ranking that required managers to allocate ratings into a forced distribution, Microsoft has created a system that gives managers more discretion to reward employees based on the merit of their contributions. Instead of a fixed distribution of bonuses, managers have more discretion to allocate rewards in a way that better reflects overall impact (while still adhering to overall budget parameters).[15]

It's easy to see the elements of bureaucracy busting in Microsoft's new approach. The old approach tended to increase unhealthy competition, reinforcing silos and the outdated set of norms and expectations. In a memo to employees, then CHRO Lisa Brummel explained, "This is a fundamentally new approach to performance and development designed to promote new levels of teamwork and agility for breakthrough business impact." The goal is to elevate teamwork and collaboration with an emphasis on employee growth and development. Consider the importance that Nadella and team have placed on a growth mindset as a foundation to its new culture, and how this shared accountability becomes an enabler.

How Can You Leverage What You Learn?

The Microsoft and Marriott examples reinforce the importance of generating new learning. As Satya Nadella has observed, "Industry does not respect tradition—it only respects innovation"—and that requires continuous learning as the foundation for agile execution.[16]

Experimentation and learning give you options. From those options it's possible for you to identify solutions that work best. Sometimes that's a universal best practice that can be applied across the whole company, but sometimes it's finding different approaches that can be applied or adapted locally. One size need not fit all. The important point is that when you have access to the options and alternatives, you can increase the repertoire and versatility of your organization.

One of the things that stops organizational learning in its tracks is when knowledge gets bottled up, hoarded, or trapped in one location, unavailable to others around the company. In their book *If We Only Knew What We Know*, Carla O'Dell and C. Jackson Grayson recognized that while companies invest significantly in developing new knowledge and insights, they often fall short of leveraging that knowledge around the organization. As one executive said, "We have no problem generating new ideas, but they don't get shared, and they soon recede, and we're no better off."[17]

In turbulent environments where agility is paramount, no amount of knowledge or insight can keep a company moving ahead if it is not distributed where it's needed. When companies don't know what they know, they hamstring the ability to be agile.

Vail Resorts: Accelerate learning across the enterprise. Like others we have highlighted, Vail Resorts is working to constantly push the frontier of learning to use agility as a competitive advantage. Like Marriott, Vail's diverse portfolio of resort properties gives it the opportunity to experiment and search for new ideas. Because each of the resorts has distinctive qualities, they have the opportunity to adapt to local situations, to test, learn, and evolve. Variation across the portfolio fuels innovation by providing Vail insights into possibilities and a potentially richer set of practices. Because Rob Katz and team have invested in best-in-class data analytics, the company can test its ideas and determine—empirically—which ones are most worthy, which ones deliver results, and which do not.

Actively manage risk. Katz has been working to maintain a "can-do" attitude of a startup, which means actively managing risk. "The goal is constantly coming up with new ideas, knowing that most of them will never get done." In his view, the key is to embrace two somewhat opposing disciplines at the same time. "One is to take a risk, but the other is to move on and realize not everything is going to go well. And not to compound mistakes. . . . The agility piece is big," said Katz. "You're going to make a mistake. The question is what you do after that mistake. How up front are you about it? What do you do afterwards?" Katz's philosophy is that when something doesn't work out, incur the cost once but then leverage the learning across the entire organization. And when a new idea does work out, that's where the company accelerates.

Share the learning. Sharing insights, innovations, and the occasional misstep, Vail works to share knowledge broadly and rapidly. "We can work together and benefit from one another's knowledge and how we can use data to assess our biggest challenges and then learn from one another," Mark Gasta said. The experience became formalized in a few best-practice groups, and it has accelerated within the organization. "All of a sudden now we have best-practice groups across all aspects of our business."

Vail Resorts' approach to knowledge sharing balances global best practice and local customization. "We have to be very responsive based on what's going on in those particular resorts," said Gasta. "Leaders inside that resort location have that ability to move on the fly with what's happening there, and benefit from the support of being a part of this larger enterprise."

Vail isn't unique in its efforts to support knowledge sharing. And a variety tools and technologies help facilitate the process. Like any capability, we can break it down into the people, processes, systems, and structures that support knowledge transfer. After action reviews, for example, were originally developed by the U.S. military to help structure a post-hoc debrief process to analyze why events occurred and how things can be done better in the future. Communities of practice and other affinity groups can help complement formal business structures by creating horizontal networks of shared interest and exchange. Each of these is supported by knowledge management portals, collaborative software, groupware, and the like.

Quite likely your experience is like ours, in that the key challenge is typically not the choice of methodologies per se, but how they are applied. Generally speaking, the first requirement is to scope the efforts correctly, managing the balance between "push" (information sent out) and "pull" (information brought in), and making it easy for others to access the information they need. Perhaps most critical is helping others to translate, refine, or adapt the knowledge to their circumstances where appropriate. Sometimes knowledge and best practice can be simply replicated in another setting. But often not. The excuse of "We're different" isn't just a cop-out. Vast repositories of valuable knowledge get stuck and isolated, never making the successful transfer to new applications because they can't be deciphered from the unique context of their origins.

That's why we would again (and again) emphasize the importance of collaboration across the enterprise to help accelerate shared learning and reintegrate it into other parts of the organization. With the right support, it is possible to dramatically steepen learning curves to transfer knowledge into new locations, situations, and applications.

BUILD DYNAMIC CAPABILITY

So far in this chapter, we've discussed two of the three major requirements for agility: situational awareness and organizational learning. Situational awareness gives you deeper insights into your customers, a better sense of the dynamic business ecosystem, and a wider view of peripheral concerns and opportunities. Better situational awareness helps prepare the organization and mitigate blind spots.

Organizational learning helps you to generate, share, and apply new knowledge and ways of working that give your organization more options, more alternatives, and a better repertoire for adapting quickly to the environment. In that regard, organizational learning helps increase the versatility of the organization.

Both are important. And the third requirement for agility is building what academics call "dynamic capability," that is, the ability to reconfigure the organization's' resources—money, people, technology, and so on—in order to orchestrate rapid change. In truth, dynamic capability is not independent from situational awareness and organizational learning; in fact it depends on them. Without good situational awareness and the capacity for organizational learning, it is impossible to effectively reshape the organization's assets in ways that improve responsiveness. In that regard, the capacity to bring about change is itself a capability. And in agile environments, it is a core capability.[18]

As we go through this section, add the following questions to the ones you've asked previously:

- How "change ready" is our organization? Do we respond to change well?
- What are the key levers we use to mobilize change? What leads, what lags, and what drags?
- In what way do our core capabilities give us a foundation for responding quickly?

How Do You Rapidly Mobilize Your Organization?

A recent McKinsey study found that "dynamic resource reallocation"— shifting money, talent, and management attention to where they will deliver the most value—was the strongest predictor of total returns to shareholders. This makes sense, and is especially important for agile execution. Getting the necessary resources in place, in a timely manner, can either make the organization nimble and productive or leave it lumbering and ineffectual. It is the essence of dynamic capability.

What was interesting about the McKinsey study was that companies in the sample weren't very good at dynamic reallocation. On average, firms reallocated only 8 percent of capital from one year to the next. And a third only reallocated 1 percent. All the while, senior executives (83 percent) identified it as the top management lever for spurring performance.[19]

The evidence is pretty clear. Sull and colleagues found less than one-third of managers believe that their organizations reallocate funds to the right places quickly enough to be effective. The reallocation of people is even worse. Only 20 percent of managers say their organizations do a good job of shifting people across units to support strategic priorities. And as a result, resources are often trapped in unproductive uses.[20]

Part of the challenge is that reallocation is a two-sided process. Resources have to be freed up from existing uses and then reallocated to new ones. Or, as CEB/Gartner sees it, companies have to practice both addition and subtraction. While companies in turbulent environments may have difficulty determining where to place their new bets, they have a very difficult time giving up on old ones. Both are hard decisions.

Companies struggle to disinvest. And there are real costs as well as opportunity costs for not doing so. Underinvesting in the future compromises the organization's capability, which multiplies over time, putting them potentially further behind and playing catch up. But failing to disinvest also wastes resources on unproductive pursuits. When does patience turn into the gambler's fallacy of one more bet before the payoff?[21]

Get the decision process right. Business and functional heads need to make the hard calls about what initiatives to cut to free capacity. And they need to have authority to make those decisions. Stated another way, managers need a "hunting license" to track new promising ventures and kill off the old ones. Because the recommendations are often proffered bottom-up from the field (recall our point about lowering the center of gravity), senior executives may not have the requisite information to make the immediate call themselves. All the more reason why the decision needs to be based on data, sound logic, and a clear analysis of the business case. Because collaboration is essential for a collective decision in these cases, curbing the natural tendency to let passion, personality, and politics influence the process is paramount.[22]

There are two more key considerations that help organizations mobilize more quickly. First, agility requires human capital flexibility. There are a couple of related approaches that help. Companies such as GE pioneered talent management systems that developed cadres of general management talent whose skills were fungible across businesses and geographies. The approach gives organizations more flexibility, especially when combined with talent reviews that integrate business necessity in the decisions (a point we'll reinforce below in our discussion of Microsoft). In addition, companies have been using contingency workers, partnerships, alliances, BPO firms, and the like to manage uneven demand and supply of human capital. The emergence of the "gig economy" is indicative of how much that has normalized as an approach for creating an agile workforce.[23]

Finally, we would again reiterate the importance of alignment around strategic intent. Recall in our chapter on Alignment, we noted that executives frequently tell us that one of their challenges is that good opportunities and priorities continually pop up. All compelling, and drawing attention—if not resources—away from the core initiatives to execute strategy. That propensity is exponentially higher in turbulent environments where agility is critical. Windows of opportunity open and close quickly, recreating perceived urgency and diverting attention. Strong alignment around a clear strategic intent helps to focus resource allocations. As much as agility may require changing the means to achieve desired ends, a clear strategic intent helps to stabilize the organization during change.

In all likelihood, organizations are faced with the challenges of organizational ambidexterity, that is, working to ensure profitable performance in the current business while investing in growth prospects that define a different future. Uncomfortable tradeoffs are inevitable, but reinforcing alignment in the leadership team helps to guide the organization through the process.[24]

Microsoft: Improve your ambidexterity. Microsoft has been working to be more nimble in realigning its resources to drive execution. And it faces the challenges of an "ambidextrous" approach to investment, making certain to continuously improve current products and services that customers depend on today while also investing more in a mobile-first and cloud-first future.

Financial resources. To ground this effort, the executive team did a thorough analysis of the macro trends in the industry (e.g., shift to the cloud, mobility) and the big opportunities ahead with each of those trends. There was great consensus on each of the trends, but not great alignment of financial investment. The key question, as Scott Guthrie put it, was, "What percentage of our overall R&D investment is focused on these trends that we all seem to agree 100 percent on?"

To ensure agility, Microsoft has a number of touch points at different intervals. The executive team combines its annual fiscal year planning process with quarterly and monthly forecasting, evaluating how the company is against plan, just like any other company would do and its shareholders would expect.

Decision making. Microsoft's approach to decision making is based on the premise that agility first depends on alignment, and then on according some discretion to the business leads. Guthrie explained, "We've got the areas that are aligned together, organized together, and execute with a great deal of autonomy while at the same time contributing to the overall Microsoft strategy. But we try to make sure that not every decision has to go through the Microsoft senior leadership team because, just for the number of businesses we're in, there's just no way we can scale." To keep connections among the independent businesses, recall from our chapter on Alignment that Nadella and team meet every week to do strategy reviews, product reviews, and execution reviews, all together as a group. In addition to helping to ensure ongoing (re)alignment, "We've been able to build agility into the system because we never go more than six days from identifying an issue to figuring out what we're going to do about it."

Organization structure. Further into the organizations, Guthrie emphasized the benefit of using smaller teams in order to improve nimbleness. "Historically at Microsoft we often had teams that were very big that would own many, many different businesses. Even the way some of our senior leaders had grown up, you measured your success based on revenue or overall business impact. That works really well when you're in a mature business and your goal is to grow by some small percentage." But Guthrie knew that disruptive change, like a shift to the cloud, required a different architecture. "After we got alignment, we moved from very big teams managed by senior people to much smaller teams." He flattened out the structure and went from a handful of direct reports to more than twenty-five at one point. Guthrie said, "Let's create some single-threaded teams, laser focused on a critical objective, and put the best people—in some cases the most senior people—in some of

TABLE 6.1 Agility Checklist

AGILITY CHECKLIST	
Situational Awareness	1. We develop deep knowledge of our customers to anticipate their future needs.
	2. We thoroughly understand the ecosystem of our industry and how the relationships are evolving.
	3. We monitor peripheral events and signals in the remote environment to look for emerging trends.
Organizational Learning	4. We empower the organization to own and solve problems, take manageable risk, and bring collective expertise.
	5. We undertake many small experiments to learn quickly and generate new avenues for growth and innovation.
	6. We make sure that what we learn in one part of the organization is shared broadly with others.
Dynamic Capability	7. We have developed very good "change readiness" to respond well to the environment.
	8. We have built a flexible organization that is able to reallocate resources quickly.
	9. We have a strong set of core capabilities that gives us the power to accelerate change.

© Scott A. Snell and Kenneth J. Carrig

Develop Situational Awareness

How is your organization's situational awareness? How deeply do you know your customers so you can anticipate where their future needs and desire may take you? How thoroughly do you understand the dynamics of your business ecosystem, particularly how they might be changing? What are the faint signals, emerging trends in the periphery, that might influence—even define—the future? When we ask executives about what keeps them up at night, these are the questions they ask themselves.

In this chapter we gave you some examples and approaches for building better situational awareness, seeing with more acuity and with a better field of vision. Attending to the future helps you prepare for what might be, if not what will be. That's a starting point, a prerequisite for agility, giving you more degrees of freedom and a better prospect of not being caught unawares.

Empower Organizational Learning

Jack Welch, former CEO of GE, once said, "An organization's ability to learn, and translate that learning into action rapidly, is the ultimate competitive advantage." In this chapter, we have hopefully given you a better perspective of how organizations generate, share, and integrate new knowledge that helps them respond more quickly and effectively to the environment. We emphasize again that empowering a broad base of the organization and lowering the center of gravity help you harness the full potential of your organization in the learning process. Giving employees an opportunity to try new things, to customize locally, to have more cycles of improvement—even at the risk of an occasional mistake—is an investment in learning. And that investment increases both the portfolio of options from which the organization can consider, as well as the versatility of the organization to respond in different ways.

So ask yourself, have you done enough to create an adaptive and versatile learning organization? As we noted at the beginning of the chapter, some of the symptoms of agility problems stem from being too focused on what's right in front of you and falling victim to "threat rigidity" in the face of change. Organizations that invest in developing a learning culture help to ameliorate these problems and set the course for better agile execution.

Build Dynamic Capability

Finally, with good situational awareness and a versatile learning organization, can your business pivot quickly, reallocate resources, and focus investment where it needs to go? Or is your story too reminiscent of the tragedy of the *Titanic*?

Is your organization asking these questions?

- Are we change ready?
- Is our leadership and talent base capable of moving quickly to new initiatives?
- Have we developed the clarity of decision making to facilitate responsiveness?
- Is our organization architecture enabling decisions and resource flow?
- Do we have alignment that gives us stability in the midst of change?

Dynamic capability requires that you reconfigure the organization's resources—money, people, technology, and so on—in order to orchestrate rapid change. It is the culmination of the other elements of agile execution.

WHAT NEXT? PUTTING IT ALL TOGETHER

As we've worked our way through the 4A framework, it's perhaps become more obvious how Alignment, Ability, Architecture, and Agility are connected and mutually reinforcing. Each plays a unique role in supporting execution capability, and they complement one another in building an overall system. In the next chapter, we bring them all together, begin the process of helping you synthesize what you've learned and start to set in place a plan to apply the learning to your organization.

7 USING THE 4A FRAMEWORK
A Guide for Action

THE 4A MODEL helps frame the challenges of execution and the most important requirements for achieving breakthrough performance. Unpacking Alignment, Ability, Architecture, and Agility in the preceding chapters helped us delve more deeply into the underlying concepts and practices that can lift an organization's capacity. It also highlighted the experience of executive teams, particularly the lessons learned along the way to better performance. However, while executives often find the 4A framework compelling, it is not uncommon for them to ask us how best to put it into practice: "What can I do to apply this to my organization—where do I start?"

The essence of execution is focused action. Much of what we've described in this book is the effort of CEOs and their teams to wrestle with complexity, clarify purpose, and focus energy on their firm's top priorities. Alignment rests on that principle. So does Ability, Architecture, and Agility. Each in their own way depends on concentrating resources in the places where it will be most useful to drive performance.

It is an unending process that requires constant attention. Larry Bossidy and Ram Charan described execution as a *discipline*, and we wholeheartedly agree. More than mere tactics, execution is the fundamental bridge between strategy and performance. It must be approached as a systematic process for rigorously reviewing and challenging strategic imperatives, operational directives, underlying capabilities, accountabilities, and performance outcomes. When managed as a disciplined process, execution is an iterative, adaptive, and robust method for running a business. Without this discipline—this systematic process—the lessons of execution might remain only good ideas left sitting on a bookshelf.[1]

In this chapter, we lay out a three-step approach for engaging others to improve execution capability (shown in Figure 7.1 below). It has been somewhat surprising how few organizations undertake the important work to clarify this sequence and to approach it methodically. As we noted back in Chapter 1, most executives acknowledge that they do not have a systematic approach for assessing their preparedness or identifying key priorities for investing in execution capability. As one senior executive noted, "We have no integrative process that ties the 4As together." Another observed, "I had no course, there is no book that tells you how to do this. We had to learn it over time as we went forward."

Our goal is to help you see the process more clearly so you can approach it in a more explicit way. Remember, execution is a collective challenge, a form of organizational change, so don't try to mastermind the design of the process by yourself in splendid isolation. Engage others and develop the approach together. The first step is setting the business context, ensuring clarity about your strategy, financial objectives, competitive positioning, and operating plan. The second step is an organizational capability assessment and deeper analysis of underlying "enablers," to help you see where execution strengths and potential problems might lie. And then, finally, the third step is establishing a game plan for taking concrete actions to improve execution.

Many leadership teams want to jump directly to the action-planning phase. Don't make that mistake. Investing time in each step provides the foundation you need to create a truly robust approach to execution.

This chapter outlines each step and provides tools you can use to create a customized action plan for your company. Recall that our overriding priorities are to profile the business context in ways that are usable by the CEO and other leadership teams, provide rapid diagnostics

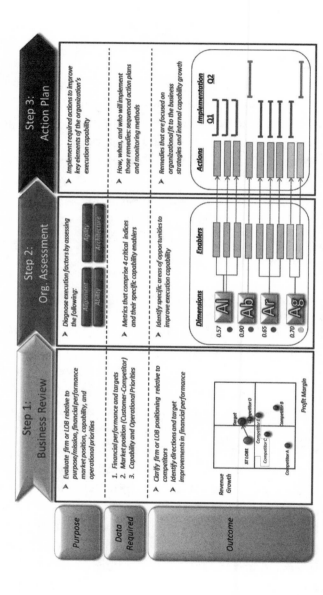

FIGURE 7.1 Improving Execution Capability

of execution capability, and prioritize targeted interventions to address capability gaps.

STEP 1: USE BUSINESS REVIEW TO SET CONTEXT

To contextualize your efforts to improve execution and performance, we recommend first engaging in a thorough assessment and review of the business. Why? Because context matters. It's a bit like talking with someone about improving physical fitness. If you asked a friend the best way to get in shape, they are likely to respond, "In order to do what?" What sport are you playing? At what level? Who's your opponent? Your best approach depends on what you want to achieve.

For that reason, our advice is to use the business review as a set of lenses to see execution more clearly and make discussions about improving capability and performance more real. As generalizable and intuitive as the 4A framework might be, our experience is that the concepts and practices have more utility when they are grounded in the context of "where the organization is now, where it wants to go, and what it needs to get there." The assessment of current and desired state has as much to do with evaluating strategic goals as it does with performance, and requires positioning within the competitive set.

Of course the "north star" in most all of these discussions is the purpose and long-term mission of the enterprise. Underneath that is a frank discussion of whether the organization is doing the right things on behalf of shareholders and customers. To that end, most executive teams tend to gravitate toward three key issues that are typically part of their business reviews:

- What's our economic imperative, that is, the organization's financial situation and longer-term aspirational targets?
- What's our market position, relative to competitors, and the value we bring to customers (and other stakeholders)?
- What are our current capabilities, and to what degree are they sufficient to achieve our goals?

Reviewing each of these assessments gives you a running start at evaluating the requirements for execution, hashing out any changes needed, and using this as an opportunity to reinforce your organization's near-term operational priorities, initiatives, resource requirements, and performance metrics. Note that the goal here is *not* to change your strategy, or even your operational plans, but to reconvene key players who have a point of view on where the organization is and where it should be headed. This type of "gap analysis" sets the context for execution requirements.

What Is Your Economic Imperative?

Let's dig a little deeper. How do you operationalize breakthrough performance? What does success look like for shareholders? We emphasize that the first step is making a realistic assessment of current and desired financial performance for the business (or each business unit). Typically, we focus on two primary financial drivers: revenue growth and operating margin (two key factors determining free cash flow and firm valuation). These factors are inevitably compared over time and relative to key competitors.

Focusing on growth and margin over time, but also relative to competitors, helps frame a discussion that allows the organization to agree on the path forward. Examining the competitive landscape in this fashion will allow the organization's leaders to engage in discussions that will drive alignment on what the organization needs to achieve.

Executive teams vary in their approach to these decisions, striking the balance between growth and margin. For example, following its acquisition of Starwood, Marriott faced challenges of rapid growth as it became the largest hotel chain in the world. But it also needed to focus on finding synergies across the enterprise and taking cost out of the business model. SunTrust's execution story was different, following the financial crisis of 2008. Rather than focusing on growth alone, CEO Bill Rogers emphasized improving efficiencies, operating margins, and profitability. Despite its smaller size compared to rivals, the bank achieved market-leading performance in shareholder value over a five-year span. Looking toward the future, and its merger with BB&T, growth may become a higher priority.

How Are You Positioned?

While the economics of the business and associated financial imperatives typically have primacy, strategy execution depends directly on
decisions about customer and competitive positioning, and potentially
decisions about other stakeholders as well. Whether in new or existing
markets, the positioning involves two fundamental considerations.

First, how are you going to win the game you're currently playing?
Enhanced positioning involves extending or expanding the current value
proposition for customers. For example, SunTrust redefined its value
proposition for customers, focusing on a broader purpose of financial
well-being and "bringing the whole bank" through cross-pollination
of its various channels. A variant of this approach is simply preserving
and reinforcing a valued position gained over time, in effect keeping
promises to customers, while pursuing more expansive financial goals.
For example, as UPS and Marriott executed their strategies for growth,
their executive teams took a series of precautions to avoid diluting the
brand, diminishing quality, and (unwittingly) destroying value. Executing against this position requires strengthening capabilities and building deeper expertise in existing domains.

Second, how are you going to change the game? *Disruptive positioning* involves changing what's possible and/or available to customers
relative to competitors. For example, some would say that Vail Resorts
redefined the ski industry with its Epic Pass, providing customers access
to a broad portfolio of ski resorts around the world and eclipsing what
any other competitor could provide. Executing against this position requires leveraging existing capabilities but also developing expertise and
new capabilities in new domains. It involves, as Joseph Schumpeter put
it, "the doing of new things or doing of things that are already being
done in a new way."[2]

These two positions are of course not mutually exclusive. In fact, we
have noted in our chapter on Agility that firms increasingly recognize
the need to do both simultaneously, and organizational "ambidexterity" is often a requirement for execution. Recall how Microsoft, for example, focuses on driving results in its current desktop businesses while

making substantial investments in building capability in cloud computing and mobile services. Both are important and are no longer tradeoffs, but complementary elements of its portfolio. Nadella and team
are steadfast in their belief that Microsoft's recent successes, and market
leading position, are the result of this approach.

In the end, the juxtaposition of current performance relative to future goals is a starting point for execution. And two other points are
relevant here.

What Is Your Operating Model?

In our chapter on Architecture, we emphasized the importance of clarifying your business operating model in order to create a "blueprint" for
strategy execution. We won't repeat that discussion here. But we will reiterate that the underlying processes, structures, systems, and skills are
the foundation of your operating model. They help define the underlying elements of your strategy and set the requirements for execution.

By devoting adequate time to this review, your team will have a
chance to reevaluate where operational priorities lie, how resources
should be allocated, and which decisions and investments matter
most. This effort is useful for three reasons. First, it is a reality check on
whether the business aspirations are realistic (in a given time frame).
Second, it helps to focus the agenda on which execution capabilities
might be missing, and sets the stage for further discussion about required investments. And third, it establishes context for all ongoing
discussions about execution. Don't forget that business performance is
the goal. Execution capability and the 4A framework are a means to get
there.

In our experience, this business review leads to a robust exchange
within the management team, which is often necessary for establishing
the priorities for execution. Not surprisingly, the process both benefits
from—and improves—alignment within the organization. In those instances where strong alignment already exists within the management
team, it is easier to establish consensus on key issues, direction, and
strategic intent, allowing the team to focus on the requirements for execution. And where initial differences exist in the team, the process can

"Great processes and average people will beat great people with mediocre processes—any day." We think he might have been missing the point. Improving Ability *and* Architecture could help turbocharge the organization.

This brings up one other trend. When improvements occur among the four dimensions, they can complement and strengthen one another. For example, a streamlined Architecture frees up talent to focus on the most important issues, leveraging their skills to more productive pursuits. Clarifying roles and decision rights helps to create a more efficient Architecture *and* achieve better Alignment. All of these improve the prospects that an organization can move with Agility. You get the point. And we've said it before; Alignment, Ability, Architecture, and Agility work as a system.

Based on this analysis and discussion of the Execution Capability Profile for their organization, executives can gain insight into the following questions:

- In which of the four areas do we have significant capability? Can that capability be used to help build areas where we don't have as much strength?
- Which areas do we need to monitor the most given that they could slide into Disqualified?
- Which areas do we need to address right away? And what is the sequence of actions we should take?

Ken's former boss at Continental Airlines, CEO Gordon Bethune, said organizations are like watches. Each component must do its part to deliver on the "one thing"; that is, telling time. If only one element fails, the entire system fails. Decreased functionality can impair the entire workings of the watch. Sometimes, even the tiniest screw that holds the mainspring on or the escapement together can be that critical.

While organizational systems are probably not as fragile as a watch, the analogy is apt. All the parts must work together for excellent execution. This reality stood front and center as we developed the 4A Framework. Alignment, Architecture, Ability, and Agility are all interconnected.

So what's the point here? Unfortunately, many companies fail to "put it all together" and take a balanced approach to executing strategy. Instead, they operate more like a whack-a-mole game, shifting resources randomly to the most "urgent," yet not necessarily most important activities. At a time of unprecedented economic and market change, it is easy to see how this can happen in organizations.

What Patterns Do You See in the Data?

While self-assessment is a valuable step in diagnosing execution capability, the approach can be supplemented with other supporting data commonly available in your organization. In today's environment, fairly exploding with big data, many organizations are identifying metrics and developing dashboards in an effort to use predictive analytics to gain insight into the four dimensions of execution.

Although the survey data is often sufficient for diagnosing potential priorities, executive teams often find it useful to review patterns in other quantitative data supported by a set of more objective metrics. That's a good idea for two reasons. First, building a metrics model from targeted data helps to operationalize the 4A framework. And when organizations have multiple lines of business, they can compare and contrast indices across those business units. Second, data analytics often can give you a view into performance issues with more granularity. For example, your assessment of Ability factors may include a concern about the leadership pipeline or talent capacity. Objective data might not only back up that conclusion; it also would give you more concrete evidence of the scope or location of the problem.

We have found that, in many cases, these data already exist within your organization. The challenge is that they typically are not aggregated in one place, one function, one database, or even one information system. For that reason, we advocate that executive teams devote time needed to establish a platform that brings these related indicators of execution capability together. Doing so provides a scorecard for evaluating current capability as well as follow-on decisions and priorities for action.

It is often useful to create a composite of the data or a predictive execution index (PEI) for your firm and/or business unit(s). As illustrated in Figure 7.4 below, each of the 4A enablers can be operationalized by a set of common internal metrics, the specifics of which depend on your business. Similar to the three rating zones for the self-assessment, your PEI should establish an upper and lower bound on each of the metrics (e.g., color coded as green, yellow, red). Aggregating across these metrics, each business receives a rating that is then conveyed as a PEI. The value of this approach is that it provides a summary indicator of execution capability and a measure of how likely that business unit will be able to achieve its goals. More prescriptively, your PEI also provides a way to probe more deeply into the root causes of any performance gaps.

There is no silver bullet, no single index that works for every situation. However, there are several alternative ways to quantify where your organization currently stands with regard to execution capability. At the end of the day, this assessment is a critical midpoint in the process between the business review and action planning. It not only helps your team assess where you are, but it will also help you establish alignment on the key priorities for improvement.

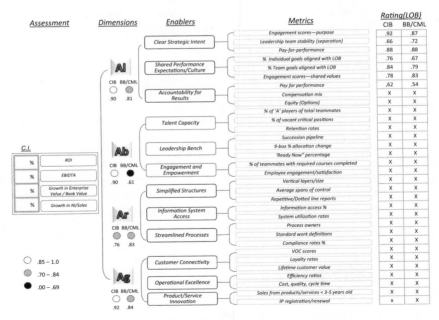

FIGURE 7.4 Predictive Execution Index (PEI) (for illustration only)

STEP 3: TAKING ACTION

The final step in implementing the 4A framework is establishing an action plan for targeted interventions. When done right, these plans serve as a "playbook" for the executive team to close the gap on execution capability. They also provide concrete guidance that allows others within the organization to take action to implement planned interventions.

The challenge at this stage is to make these plans both holistic and actionable. We recommend shining a consistent light on the following principles:

- *Contextual:* The key priorities of the plan must derive from and support your business review. It should clearly align with "where you are, and where you want to go."
- *Integrated:* The plan must both take into consideration the business plan and address each of the four A's, individually and as an integrated system. All metrics that tie performance to intervention areas should be defined in a way that allows ongoing assessment and trend analysis.
- *Sequenced:* Remember to stage your interventions in a way that the steps are additive and reinforce each other. Agree on timelines for action and review. Make each step very clear, taking care of remedial issues first, quickly, and addressing priority issues with highest impact. The momentum will help carry subsequent interventions to get the most from them as well.
- *Resourced:* To achieve the lift you're looking for, identify owners of each intervention or initiative. Then budget for all the required resources (financial, human, information, time).
- *Disciplined*: This is not merely a "once-and-done" planning process. The key is to establish a methodical approach and cadence whereby the leadership team applies, reviews, and adapts the action plans on an ongoing basis.

Ensuring that these principles are met helps you establish a governance process that maximizes your chances for success and that your interventions will have optimal impact. Our short-hand rubric for review is to continually check the "why, what, how, who, when" questions.

- *Why?* Your rationale for action and intervention needs to be clearly connected to the business case for performance. Make sure the outcomes needed are made clear.
- *What?* The priorities for actions, what you'll do, and what difference it will make need to be laid out in some detail. Connect actions to outcomes.
- *How?* Be clear about how you'll undertake these interventions. The approach needs to be laid out in detail, not just generalities.
- *Who?* Make certain that you clarify who will take action and who is accountable.
- *When?* Short- and long-term timelines need to connect actions, outputs, and impact.

Are Your Priorities Clear?

Lewis Carrol once observed, "If you don't know where you are going, any road will take you there." We would drive home the point that your action plans not only need to make your priorities crystal clear, they also need to connect actions to desired outcomes. Figure 7.5, for example, shows priorities for action, targeted interventions, and timelines for implementation. Priorities are driven by 4A scoring during the capability assessment stage. Your organizational self-assessment and corroborating analytics will show which areas are most pressing.

Note in this example, the overall trouble spot is Agility. But beyond that one dimension, your assessment also will show perhaps more specific enablers underlying the capability that need to be addressed. Understand the whole system. In areas where your organization is Disqualified (red zone), taking remedial action is both urgent and important. Before planned interventions in other areas will likely pay off, these trouble spots have priority. And we might also note that because of the larger performance gap, the timeline for intervention likely will be longer.

For each of the 4A dimensions and each underlying enabler, your team will devise specific targeted actions to address the performance issue. For example, in this case, focusing on customer relationship management was seen as a key factor in developing better situational

Action Plan: Interventions

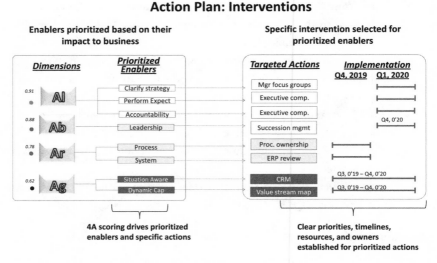

Enablers prioritized based on their impact to business		Specific intervention selected for prioritized enablers	

4A scoring drives prioritized enablers and specific actions

Clear priorities, timelines, resources, and owners established for prioritized actions

FIGURE 7.5 Action Plan Interventions (for illustration only)

awareness to support Agility. Your team will need to determine the appropriate sequencing of these interventions, varying the length of time, as well as initiation and delivery dates. Remember that Alignment, Agility, Architecture, and Ability are only *conceptually* distinct. In practice, they reinforce one another and constitute an integrated system.

Who Owns Execution?

The "why, what, and how" of these action plans is critical, but so is the "who." Who is responsible? We continue to be perplexed that execution, and interventions to improve it, are often rapidly delegated from the leadership team to others in the organization.

That's a mistake. Leaders need to own execution. We've asked senior leaders, "Who is the chief execution officer?" and they often look around. In some cases, it might be the COO. But more often, the answer is "We are." At the end of the day, the overall leadership team is on the hook to make sure the organization executes well and has the capacity to drive performance breakthroughs. For that reason, they should also own the action plan.

But do they? Yes, others are surely involved, and much of the operational elements will be directed to and implemented by others. For each step and each intervention, it is important to clarify the individual (or team) who has responsibility, authority, and accountability to execute against the plan. But the ultimate governance, ownership, and accountability belongs with the leadership team. They need to champion the efforts, make certain those efforts are properly (and sufficiently) resourced, and monitor progress toward the aspired goals.

Equally important, we would caution that the process must remain fluid with multiple touch points for review, iteration, adjustment, and course correction. Each of the CEOs we worked with in writing this book emphasized that the annual review cycle is out. Rather than a once-a-year review, they have found the need to circle back with their teams intermittently, establishing feedback loops and multiple strategic reviews throughout the year. Among other reasons, this helps to simultaneously reinforce Alignment and provide the foundation for inevitable adjustments.

CONCLUSION: THE DISCIPLINE OF EXECUTION

The bottom line is that when companies focus on key priorities, engage their leadership and entire organization around that agenda, hone the systems and culture to support it, and invest ahead of change, they achieve a step change in performance. Executives who apply these principles and practices, and are consistently vigilant in building better capability, move closer to the ideals of strategic execution.

You can do it, too. We've seen the evidence and are confident that the successes are repeatable in your organization. Our original purpose for this book—to share a useable approach that helps business leaders get a firmer grasp on the levers of execution—was based on that belief.

By first framing the challenges of execution, embracing the underlying logic of the 4A framework, and applying a set of actionable tools to address performance gaps, you and your team will gain more traction in your critical path forward. And just as important, by building a discipline around this approach and embedding it in the way you work, you will sustain positive momentum over time. In our experience, the upside potential is significant.

Through our experience with these diverse companies and executive teams, we have learned a good deal about how the components of the 4A framework combine to drive strategic execution. But, like the executives with whom we met, we recognize that tackling the execution challenge is a journey where continuous learning is paramount.

What's your next step? That answer probably varies, but hopefully the principles and practices in this book, and the stories from our five companies, have inspired and enlightened your way forward. The key to success doesn't reside with the tools. It depends on your desire to truthfully recognize your organization's current state and your commitment to drive excellence that delivers breakthrough performance. Good luck in your endeavors, and in your own journey.

APPENDIX: EXECUTION CAPABILITY DIAGNOSTIC SURVEY

Execution Capability Diagnostic Survey

Directions: Rate each item below from 1 (strongly disagree) to 5 (strongly agree)		Rating	Comments
SAMPLE	Our company is a good company.	3	We do well but there is always room for improvement.
	ALIGNMENT		
Strategic Intent	1. Our strategy is clearly understood and supported by all managers.		
	2. We have clear prioritized goals that our leaders regularly communicate throughout the enterprise.		
	3. Our executive team models all the behaviors necessary to translate our strategy into performance.		
Shared Expectations	4. Norms and expectations for high performance are shared throughout the organization.		
	5. Our culture is defined by values, behaviors, and expectations of excellence.		
	6. Our culture encourages employees to challenge and bring forth new ideas to peers and managers.		
Accountability	7. Managers are held accountable for achieving results and actions that support our strategy.		
	8. Rewards are connected to both individual and team performance.		
	9. Individuals hold themselves accountable for results and execution of strategy across the entire enterprise.		
	ABILITY		
Leadership	10. Our leaders have the skills, competencies, and experience needed for breakthrough performance.		
	11. We develop a continual flow of "next generation" leaders who are capable of leading us to the future.		
	12. Our leaders inspire and empower others to achieve organizational goals.		
Talent	13. We have a robust talent management system to identify, develop, and retain high-quality employees.		
	14. High-priority, "mission-critical" positions are filled by our top performers.		
	15. Managers spend time coaching and developing their employees and teams.		
Collaboration	16. Managers and employees work well together to make everyone better.		
	17. Teams have discretion to make decisions and act using their best judgement.		
	18. There is a spirit of collaboration that cuts across business units and functions.		

ARCHITECTURE

Clear Operating Model
19. We have clarified our operating model that connects core capability to our customer value proposition.
20. For each capability, we know which processes, systems, structures, and skills are most critical.
21. We have prioritized key areas for investment to enhance our capability system for the future.

Streamlined Organization
22. We have streamlined the organization structure to facilitate the key drivers of customer value.
23. Roles and responsibilities are well defined with clear decision rights and authorities.
24. We have created lateral connections across our structure to improve collaboration and joint decision making.

Intelligent Architecture
25. We have streamlined our core processes to improve workflow, increase productivity, and eliminate waste.
26. Information is accessible and knowledge shared throughout the organization.
27. Information systems inform and enable decision making with timely data.

AGILITY

Situational Awareness
28. We develop deep knowledge of our customers to anticipate their future needs.
29. We thoroughly understand the ecosystem of our industry and how the relationships are evolving.
30. We monitor peripheral events and signals in the remote environment to look for emerging trends.

Organizational Learning
31. We empower the organization to own and solve problems, take manageable risk, and bring collective expertise.
32. We undertake many small experiments to learn quickly and generate new avenues for growth and innovation.
33. We make sure that what we learn in one part of the organization is shared broadly with others.

Dynamic Capability
34. We have developed very good "change readiness" to respond well to the environment.
35. We have built a flexible organization that is able to reallocate resources quickly.
36. We have a strong set of core capabilities that gives us the power to accelerate change.

© Scott A. Snell and Kenneth J. Carrig

NOTE: An online version of this diagnostic survey can be found on the Stanford University Press portal at http://bit.ly/executionsurvey. The online diagnostic will provide you with customized feedback similar to Figure 7.2 on page 192.

NOTES

Chapter 1

1. D. Sull, R. Homkes, and C. Sull, "Why Strategy Execution Unravels—and What to Do About It," *Harvard Business Review* (March 2015), https://hbr.org/2015/03/why-strategy-execution-unravelsand-what-to-do-about-it.

2. M. Morgan, R. E. Levitt, and W. Malek, *Executing Strategy: How to Break It Down and Get It Done* (Boston: Harvard Business School Press, 2007).

3. J. P. Kotter, "Accelerate!" *Harvard Business Review*, November 2012.

4. G. L. Neilson, K. L. Martin, and E. Powers, "The Secrets to Successful Strategy Execution," *Harvard Business Review*, June 2008.

5. P. Rogers and M. Blenko, *The Decision-Driven Organization* (Boston: Bain and Company, 2005).

6. L. Bossidy and R. Charan, *Execution: The Discipline of Getting Things Done* (New York: Crown Publishing, 2002); S. Keller and C. Price, *Beyond Performance: How Great Organizations Build Ultimate Competitive Advantage* (Hoboken, NJ: John Wiley & Sons, 2011).

7. Morgan, Levitt, and Malek, *Executing Strategy*.

8. J. Richardson, "The Business Model: An Integrative Framework for Strategy Execution," *Strategic Change* 14, no. 5 (2008): 133–44.

9. T. J. Peters and R. H. Waterman, *In Search of Excellence: Lessons from America's Best-Run Companies* (New York: Harper and Row, 1982). In doing background research for this book, we relied on some excellent sources. Here is a short list of some of the best: Bossidy and Charan, *Execution*; W. Joyce, N. Nohria, and B. Robertson, *What Really Works: The 4+2 Formula for Sustained Business Success* (New York: Harper Business, 2003); P. Leinwand and C. Mainardi, *Strategy That Works* (Boston: Harvard Business School Press, 2016); Morgan, Levitt, and Malek, *Executing Strategy*; Keller and Price, *Beyond Performance*; C. McChesney, S. Covey, and J. Huling, *The Four Disciplines of Execution* (New York: Free Press, 2012).

10. J. W. Marriott, "Marriott's Executive Chairman on Choosing the First Nonfamily CEO," *Harvard Business Review* (May 2013), https://hbr.org/2013/05/marriotts-executive-chairman-on-choosing-the-first-nonfamily-ceo.

Chapter 2

1. D. A. Ready and E. Truelove, "The Power of Collective Ambition," *Harvard Business Review* (December 2011).

2. Harvard Business Review, "How Hierarchy Can Hurt Strategy Execution," *Harvard Business Review,* July–August, 2010.

3. R. Tetzeli, "GM Gets Ready for a 'Post Car' Future," *Fortune* (May 28, 2018).

4. M. Colias and A. Al-Musllim,. "Ford Hives Off Self-Driving Operations," *Wall Street Journal* (July 24, 2018); D. Buss, "Ford Creates 'Team Edison' to Accelerate Its Efforts in Battery-Electric Vehicles," *Forbes* (October 2, 2017).

5. D. Wiener-Bronner, "Tesla Just Became the Most Valuable Carmaker in America," *CNN Money* (April 11, 2017).

6. M. E. Porter, "What Is Strategy?" *Harvard Business Review* (November–December 1996).

7. W. Chan Kim and Renee Bauborgne, "Tipping Point Leadership," *Harvard Business Review* (2003).

8. Eliyahu M. Goldratt and Jeff Cox, *The Goal: A Process of Ongoing Improvement* (Great Barrington, MA.: North River Press, 1984).

9. J. G. Clawson, *Level Three Leadership: Getting Below the Surface* (Upper Saddle River, NJ: Pearson/ Prentice Hall, 2009); R. Cross and R. J. Thomas, "Managing Yourself: A Smarter Way to Network," *Harvard Business Review* (July–August 2011); S. G. Barsade, "The Ripple Effect: Emotional Contagion and Its Influence on Group Behavior," *Administrative Science Quarterly* December 2002).

10. T. Levitt, "Exploit the Product Life Cycle," *Harvard Business Review* (November 1965); J. Hill, "A Brief History of Nylon," *Mental Floss* (March 8, 2015).

Chapter 3

1. J. S. Bhanver, *Nadella: The Changing Face of Microsoft* (Guragon, India: Hachette, 2014); K. Eichenwald, "Microsoft's Lost Decade," *Vanity Fair*, July 24, 2014.

2. The second law of thermodynamics. For more on this topic related to organizations, see K. E. Weick, *The Social Psychology of Organizing* (Topics in Social Psychology Series) (New York: McGraw-Hill, 1979).

3. P. Leinwand and C. Mainardi, *Strategy That Works: Closing the Gap between Strategy and Execution* (Boston: Harvard Business Review Press, 2016).

4. J. Jargon, "McDonald's Decides to Embrace Fast-Food Identity," *Wall Street Journal*, March 1, 2017; J. Jargon, "McDonald's Knows It's Losing the Burger Battle—Can It Come Back?" *Wall Street Journal*, October 6, 2016; J. Jargon, "Regulars Lift McDonald's Sales," *Wall Street Journal*, April 25, 2017.

5. G. Stein, *The Art of Racing in the Rain* (New York: Harper Collins, 2009).

6. L. Bossidy and R. Charan, *Execution: The Discipline of Getting Things Done* (New York: Crown, 2002).

7. G. Yemen and S. Snell, "AstraZeneca: Transforming How New Medicines Flow to Patients." Darden Business Publishing, UVA-S-0221, 2012.

8. C. McChesney, S. Covey, and J. Huling, *The Four Disciplines of Execution* (New York: Simon & Schuster, 2012).

9. J. W. Dean, P. Brandes, and R. Dharwadkar, R., 1998. "Organizational Cynicism." *Academy of Management Review* 23, no. 2 (1998): 341–52.

10. G. Hamel and C. K. Prahalad, "Strategic Intent," *Harvard Business Review* 83, no. 7 (2005): 148–61; G. Hamel and C. K. Prahalad, C.K., 2010. *Strategic Intent* (Boston, MA: Harvard Business Review Press, 2010); C. K. Prahalad and R. A. Bettis, "The Dominant Logic: A New Linkage between Diversity and Performance," *Strategic Management Journal* 7, no. 6 (1986): 485–501. R. A. Bettis and C. K. Prahalad, "The Dominant Logic: Retrospective and Extension," *Strategic Management Journal* 16, no. 1 (1995): 5–14.

11. S. Keller and C. Price, *Beyond Performance: How Great Organizations Build Ultimate Competitive Advantage* (Hoboken, NJ: John Wiley & Sons, 2011).

12. M. Treacy and F. D. Wiersema, *The Discipline of Market Leaders: Choose Your Customers, Narrow Your Focus, Dominate Your Market* (Reading, MA: Addison-Wesley, 1995).

13. J. C. Collins, *Good to Great: Why Some Companies Make the Leap . . . and Others Don't* (New York: Random House, 2001).

14. Satya Nadella, email to employees on first day as CEO, posted February 14, 2014.

15. As Casey Kasem so often said, "Keep your feet on the ground, and keep reaching for the stars." Casey Kasem was an American disc jockey, music historian, radio personality, and host of *American Top 40*. He also provided the voice of "Shaggy" in the Scooby-Doo cartoon franchise. These are important things to know.

16. Satya Nadella, email to Microsoft employees, October 14, 2014.

17. Bossidy and Charan, *Execution*, 85.

18. L. V. Gerstner, *Who Says Elephants Can't Dance: Leading a Great Enterprise through Dramatic Change* (New York: HarperBusiness, 2002), 182.

19. A. J. Rucci, S. P. Kirn, and R. T. Quinn, "The Employee-Customer-Profit Chain at Sears," *Harvard Business Review* 76 (1998): 82–98. See also, J. L. Heskett and L. A. Schlesinger, "Putting the Service-Profit Chain to Work," *Harvard Business Review* 72, no. 2 (1994): 164–74.

20. Bossidy and Charan, *Execution*, 85.

21. C. S. Dweck, *Mindset: The New Psychology of Success* (New York: Random House Digital, 2008), Bhanver, *Nadella*; D. Bass, "Satya Nadella Talks Microsoft at Middle Age," *Bloomberg Businessweek*, August 4, 2016.

22. From David Abney speech at Thunderbird Business School.

23. P. Lencioni, *Advantage* (San Francisco: Jossey-Bass, 2012).

24. R. S. Kaplan and D. P. Norton, *The Balanced Scorecard: Translating Strategy into Action* (Boston, MA: Harvard Business School Press, 1996).

25. S. G. Barsade, "The Ripple Effect: Emotional Contagion and Its Influence on Group Behavior," *Administrative Science Quarterly* 47, no. 4 (2002): 644–75.

26. G. Bethune, *From Worst to First: Behind the scenes of Continental's Remarkable Comeback* (New York: John Wiley & Sons, 1999).

Chapter 4

1. A. Vance, "Steve Balmer Reboots," *Bloomberg Businessweek*, January 12, 2012.

2. Ocean Tomo LLC, "Annual Study of Intangible Asset Market Value," March, 5, 2015, http://www.oceantomo.com/blog/2015/03-05-ocean-tomo-2015-intangible-asset-market-value/.

3. R. Wartzman and L. Crosby, "The Key Factor Driving a Company's Results: People," *Wall Street Journal*, August 13, 2018; K. O'Leonard and S. Harris, "Talent Management Factbook 2010: Best Practices and Benchmarks in U.S. Talent Management," Bersen/Deloitte, 2010.

4. Ed Hess, *Learn or Die* (New York: Columbia University Press, 2014).

5. D. Ready and J. A. Conger, "Make Your Company a Talent Factory," Harvard Business Review, 2007.

6. D. Ancona, T. W. Malone, W. J. Orlikowski, and P. M. Senge, "In Praise of the Incomplete Leader," *Harvard Business Review* 85, no. 2 (2007); 92–100.

7. Dominic Rushe, "Satya Nadella Named Microsoft CEO as Bill Gates Steps Down as Chairman," *The Guardian*, February 4, 2014.

8. Ron Wallance, *Leadership Lessons from a UPS Driver: Delivering a Culture of We, Not Me* (Oakland, CA: Berrett-Koehler Publishers, 2016), 16.

9. Eric Lesser, Denis Brousseau, and Tim Ringo, "Focal Jobs: Viewing Talent Through a Different Lens," IBM Global Business Services Executive Reports. IMG Institute for Business Value, Human Capital Management. October 2009.

10. D. P. Lepak and S. A. Snell, "Examining the Human Resource Architecture: The Relationships among Human Capital, Employment, and Human Resource Configurations," *Journal of Management* 28, no. 4 (2002): 517–43.

11. S. C. Kang and S. A. Snell, "Intellectual Capital Architectures and Ambidextrous Learning: A Framework for Human Resource Management," *Journal of Management Studies* 46, no. 1 (2009): 65–92.

12. D. Ulrich, "Intellectual Capital = Competence x Commitment," *Sloan Management Review* 39, no. 2 (1998): 15.

13. Michael M. Lombardo and Robert W. Eichinger, *The Career Architect Development Planner* (Minneapolis, MN: Lominger, 1996).

14. R. Cross, R. Rebele, and A. Grant, "Collaborative Overload," *Harvard Business Review* (January–February 2016): 74–79.

15. J. R. Austin, "Transactive Memory in Organizational Groups: The effects of Content, Consensus, Specialization, and Accuracy on Group Performance," *Journal of Applied Psychology* 88, no. 5 (2003): 866–78. See also Daniel Wegner, Daniel. 1987. "Transactive Memory: A Contemporary Analysis of the Group Mind," in *Theories of Group Behavior*, edited by B. Mullen and G. R. Goethals (New York: Springer-Verlag, 1986), 185–208.

16. S. Cartwright and C. L. Cooper, "The Role of Culture Compatibility in Successful Organizational Marriage," *Academy of Management Executive* 7, no. 2 (1993): 57–70.

17. Deanna Ting, "Marriott CEO Interview: Buying Starwood and Its $13 Billion Bet on Loyalty," *Skift*, September 23, 2016.

Chapter 5

1. Louis Sullivan, Louis (1924). *Autobiography of an Idea* (New York: Press of the American Institute of Architects, 1924), 108.

2. W. Edwards Deming, *Out of the Crisis* (Boston: MIT Press, 1986).

3. Emile Durkheim, *The Division of Labor in Society* (New York: Simon and Schuster, 2014).

4. Gary L. Neilson, Karla L. Martin, and Elizabeth Powers, "The Secrets to Successful Strategy Execution," *Harvard Business Review* 86, no. 6 (2008): 60.

5. W. Ross Ashby, "Requisite Variety and Its Implications for the Control of Complex Systems," in *Facets of Systems Science*, ed. George J. Klir (New York: Plenum, 1991), 405–17.

6. M. Blenko, E. Garton, and L. Mottura, "Winning Operating Models That Convert Strategy to Results," Bain and Company, December 10, 2014, https://www.bain.com/insights/winning-operating-models-that-convert-strategy-to-results/.

7. M. Treacy and F. Wiersema, *The Discipline of Market Leaders: Choose Your Customers, Narrow Your Focus, Dominate Your Market* (New York: Basic Books, 1997).

8. Federal Emergency Management Agency, "Core Capabilities," https://www.fema.gov/core-capabilities.

9. Stuart A. Kauffman, "Escaping the Red Queen Effect." *McKinsey Quarterly* 1 (1995): 118–30.

10. Letter to shareholders, 2016 annual report.

11. R. Kermisch and J. Fallis, "Killing Complexity Before Complexity Kills Growth," Bain and Company, April 14, 2017, https://www.bain.com/insights/killing-complexity-before-complexity-kills-growth/.

12. A. Kates and G. Kesler, "Activating Global Operating Models: The Bridge from Organization Design to Performance," *Journal of Organization Design* 4, no. 2 (2015): 38–47.

13. Bain and Company, "Streamlining Spans and Layers," March 16, 2010, https://www.bain.com/insights/streamlining-spans-and-layers/.

14. K. J. Meier and L. J. O'Toole Jr, "Management Theory and Occam's Razor: How Public Organizations Buffer the Environment," *Administration & Society* 39, no. 8 (2008): 931–58.

15. Ballmer's July 11, 2013, memo to all Microsoft employees.

16. P. R. Lawrence and J. W. Lorsch, "Differentiation and Integration in Complex Organizations," *Administrative Science Quarterly* 12, no. 1 (1967): 1–47.

17. M. Hammer, "Reengineering Work: Don't Automate, Obliterate," *Harvard Business Review* (1990).

18. Economist Intelligence Unit, *Foresight 2020: Economic, Industry and Corporate Trends* (London: Economist Intelligence Unit, 2006).

19. L. Segal, A. Goldstein, J. Goldman, and R. Harfoush, "What UPS Drivers Can Tell Us about the Automated Future of Work," *Wired*, February 21, 2014. See also S. Rosenbush and L. Stevens, "At UPS, the Algorithm Is the Driver," *Wall Street Journal*, February 16, 2015.

20. International Data Corporation, *UPS Smart Manufacturing Survey*, January 2016. See also C. Chung, "Move Over Lean Six Sigma, Here Come Smart Operations," UPS Longitudes, November 7, 2016, https://longitudes.ups.com/smart-operations/.

21. Laurence J. Peter and Raymond Hull, *The Peter Principle: Why Things Always Go Wrong* (New York: William Morrow, 1969).

Chapter 6

1. N. N. Taleb, *Antifragile: Things That Gain from Disorder* (New York: Random House, 2012).

2. Pekka-Ala Pietilä, quoted in Olli-Pekka Kallasvuo interview, *Financial Times*, December 4, 2006.

3. Clayton Christensen, *The Innovator's Dilemma: The Revolutionary Book That Will Change the Way You Do Business* (New York; HarperBusiness, 2011).

4. B. M. Staw, L. E. Sandelands, and J. E. Dutton, "Threat Rigidity Effects in Organizational Behavior: A Multilevel Analysis," *Administrative Science Quarterly* 26, no. 4 (1981): 501–24.

5. D. Sull, R. Homkes, and C. Sull, "Why Strategy Execution Unravels—and What to Do About It," *Harvard Business Review*, 2015.

6. M. T. Hannan, and J. Freeman, "Structural Inertia and Organizational Change," *American Sociological Review* 49, no. 2 (1984): 149–64.

7. CEB/Gartner, *Growth Unlocked: Closing the Strategy-to-Execution Gap*, November 5, 2014, https://www.gartner.com/doc/3767818.

8. M. Bazigos, A. De Smet, and C. Gagnon, "Why Agility Pays," *McKinsey Quarterly*, December 2015.

9. M. R. Endsley, M.R., 1995. "Toward a Theory of Situation Awareness in Dynamic Systems," *Human Factors* 37, no. 1 (1995): 32–64.

10. W. M. Cohen and D. A. Levinthal, "Absorptive Capacity: A New Perspective on Learning and Innovation," *Administrative Science Quarterly* 35, no. 1 (1990): 128–52.

11. J. F. Moore, "Predators and Prey: A New Ecology of Competition," *Harvard Business Review* (May/June 1993).

12. George S. Day and Paul J. H. Schoemaker, *Peripheral Vision: Detecting the Weak Signals That Will Make or Break Your Company* (Boston: Harvard Business School, 2006).

13. D. Leonard-Barton, "The Factory as a Learning Laboratory," *Sloan Management Review* (Fall 1992).

14. C. G. Worley, T. Williams, and E. E. Lawler, *The Agility Factor: Building Sustainable Organizations for Superior Performance* (San Francisco: Jossey-Bass, 2014).

15. T. Warren, "Microsoft Axes Its Controversial Employee-Ranking System," *The Verge*, November 12, 2013; Julie Bort, "This Is Why Some Microsoft Employees Still Fear the Controversial 'Stack Ranking' Employee Review System," *Business Insider*, August 27, 2014; "Break Free from Performance Management Shackles: Companies That Are Paving the Way," *Business.com*, February 24, 2017.

16. Memo to Microsoft employees, "Satya Nadella Announces Changes to Senior Leadership Team," posted March 3, 2014.

17. C. O'Dell and C. Jackson Grayson, *If Only We Knew What We Know: The Transfer of Internal Knowledge and Best Practice* (New York: Free Press, 1998).

18. D. Teece, G. Pisano, and A. Shuen, "Dynamic Capabilities and Strategic Management," *Strategic Management Journal* 18, no. 7 (1997): 509–33.

19. S. Hall, D. Lovallo, and R. Musters, "How to Put Your Money Where Your Strategy Is," *McKinsey Quarterly*, March 2012.

20. Sull, Homkes, and Sull, "Why Strategy Execution Unravels."

21. Sull, Homkes, and Sull, "Why Strategy Execution Unravels."

22. D. Sull, "Competing through Organizational Agility," *McKinsey Quarterly*, December 2009; D. Sull, "How to Thrive in Turbulent Markets," *Harvard Business Review* (February 2009).

23. K. Strauss, "What Is Driving the 'Gig' Economy?" *Forbes* (February 21, 2017); see also P. M. Wright and S. A. Snell, "Toward a Unifying Framework for Exploring Fit and Flexibility in Strategic Human Resource Management," *Academy of Management Review* 23, no. 4 (October 1998): 756–72.

24. C. A. O'Reilly and M. L. Tushman, "The Ambidextrous Organization," *Harvard Business Review* (2004).

25. C. Argyris and D. A. Schön, *Organizational Learning: A Theory of Action Perspective* (Reading, MA: Addison-Wesley, 1978).

Chapter 7

1. L. Bossidy and R. Charan, *Execution: The Discipline of Getting Things Done* (New York: Crown Business, 2002).

2. J. A. Schumpeter, "The Creative Response in Economic History," *Journal of Economic History* 7 (1947): 149–59.

INDEX

Page numbers followed by f or t indicate material in figures or tables.